RECLAIMING *the* GREAT COMMISSION

A Roadmap to Parish Health

FR. EVAN ARMATAS

ANCIENT FAITH PUBLISHING

CHESTERTON, INDIANA

Published by:
   Ancient Faith Publishing
   A Division of Ancient Faith Ministries
   P.O. Box 748
   Chesterton, IN 46304

ISBN: 978-1-955890-29-8

Library of Congress Control Number: 2022942345

Printed in the United States of America

*To those who serve the Lord and His Church
and to those I have served,
who have taught me so much.*

Contents

Foreword

I GREW UP in an evangelical Christian home. As a thirteen-year-old boy, I attended church camp at Camp Hickory in Round Lake, Illinois. It was a two-week summer program, and my friends and I were assigned to Camp Potawatomi, a cabin in the woods. The counselor at our particular cabin announced that he wanted to have one-on-one meetings with us before camp began. We didn't know what the agenda was, but fortunately my name was Maddex, and my friend's name was Olson. Since the counselor was going alphabetically, we had time to grill the A-through-L campers about his agenda. It was twofold. First, he wanted to find out if we were saved. Second, he wanted to know if we were witnessing our faith to our friends in school.

Well, I had that first one pretty well covered. I knew that I knew that I knew that I was born again. I had walked the aisle. I had accepted Christ as my personal Savior according to everything that I was taught in church and in my home. I was a Christian. So I wasn't too worried about that part. What scared me to death was the second part: Are you faithfully witnessing your faith to people in school?

When my time came, the counselor sat me down and said, "John, I have two questions for you. Are you saved?" I gave all the right answers.

"Second question. How many kids have you witnessed to in your class in the last two weeks?"

"Well," I said, "I don't actually talk about my faith. I'm more of a silent witness."

He replied, "And just what does a silent witness mean?"

There was no category in my church upbringing for "silent witness." It was all about the numbers. How many had we "led to the Lord"? How many doorbells did we ring on Thursday night visitation?

So, when my wife, Tonya, and I became Orthodox, it took me a little while to understand what evangelism meant in the Holy, Catholic, and Apostolic Church. I knew what evangelism was as an evangelical Christian, but I didn't hear a lot about it as an Orthodox Christian.

Naturally, I asked questions about evangelism in Orthodoxy. I heard things like "We don't do that," or "That's Protestant." Perhaps the most pious-sounding explanation was, "We just tell people to 'come and see.'" But if "come and see" is the acceptable and approved method, how do we interpret Jesus' Great Commission in Matthew 28:19–20 to "go therefore and make disciples of all the nations, baptizing them in the name of the Father and of the Son and of the Holy Spirit, teaching them to observe all things that I have commanded you"? Or Mark 16:15, where He tells us, "Go into all the world and preach the gospel to every creature"? Notice the active verbs: *Go. Baptize. Teach. Preach.*

Saint John Chrysostom said, "I do not believe in the salvation of anyone who does not believe in the salvation of others." So what does the Great Commission mean in the Orthodox Church today? And if our parishes have lost sight of it, how can we reclaim it?

Father Andrew Damick wrote about what it means to be apostolic in his blog post, "Are All Orthodox Christians Supposed to Evangelize?" (August 4, 2017):

8

I can't stand it when *apostolic* is reduced to a badge of authenticity rather than seen for what it is—a command to go forth.

Good news is *news*—that means going and talking, not simply waiting around for people to show up. Any method of Church life that basically encourages people to treat the Gospel as a private possession is fundamentally treasonous to the Kingdom.

Yes, I am indeed kind of mad about the fact that we don't imitate our own saints very much in this regard.

It may be that not all of us are called to be apostles, but we are indeed all called to be apostolic—or we are not in the Church. We may just as easily say that not all of us are called to be one or holy or catholic—which is of course nonsense.

So what about our apostolic heritage as Orthodox Christians? Saint Innocent of Alaska was a nineteenth-century missionary hero who traveled many miles in very rough terrain and at great peril to himself to go visit and dwell among a people who were totally foreign to him and to his culture. But we have to ask ourselves, Why? What was the point? Why did he make that journey? Why did he sacrifice so much for these people?

He could just as easily have sent them letters and said, "The next time you're in Russia, stop by and visit us at vespers. You'll love it. It's worship like you've never seen before." That's often our message to people today in our country, right? "Come and see. Come and visit. You need to experience the service."

Believe me, I do embrace that invitation. Nothing grabbed me more than my first vespers service in English, where I experienced worship that was bathed in the psalms and the prayers. It was riveting. I am not minimizing the importance of "come and see." I'm saying instead:

Let's not make that approach the default for our evangelism efforts.

In *Reclaiming the Great Commission*, Fr. Evan takes on the Great Commission in the context of parish renewal and revitalization, and he does so with the reminder that change must begin with us. Evangelism is not a numbers game. It's not a trophy cabinet. It is lived as well as spoken and written. We want to be saved because we love our Lord. We want to see others saved because we love them.

We need to repent. We need to be transformed. In short, *we* need to be saved. Not just yesterday or today, but every day. Our inner renewal will spill over into our parishes. It will change our mindset from preserving a culture to saving the world. From focusing on nonessentials to focusing on Christ and the gospel.

Read and share this book with your priest and others in your parish. Use the reviews at the end of each chapter to help you actualize what you've learned.

We don't have to settle for stagnant or spiritually vacuous parishes in Orthodoxy. Our society is hungry for rooted, vibrant, genuine, and life-giving communities that show the love of Christ and that welcome the sick and infirm into our hospital so that we can heal together.

John Maddex
CEO of Ancient Faith Ministries

Introduction

Meeting Father Elias

THERE HAVE BEEN MOMENTS in my time as a priest when I was reminded of the famous quote—the origin of which remains uncertain—that states, "Laws are like sausages. It's better not to see them being made." Seeing the processes behind the curtain often robs us of our rose-colored-glasses view of the world.

Such a glimpse can also be highly enlightening. Many years ago, as a new priest, I attended my first Clergy–Laity Congress for my metropolis. Because I was serving in the host community, I was involved with the planning and had many conversations with the guests. One of them was a former Episcopal clergyman, Fr. Elias, who had recently been ordained an Orthodox priest.

My opportunity to speak with this man did not come until after our business meeting. At the end of that meeting, I was concerned. We had spent well over two hours going over minor details: forms, funding allocations, and the minutiae of parish operations. Given the banality of our discussion, I feared this former Episcopalian would run screaming back to his old church.

After sheepishly introducing myself to him and welcoming him to the Greek Orthodox Metropolis of Denver, I asked him about his first impressions. What he said to me has stayed with me and undergirds my current message.

"Well," he said, "that was the best clergy meeting I ever attended!"

I asked him if he was kidding.

"No," he said, "but you have to understand, I've spent the past thirty years defending the divinity of Christ in clergy meetings. None of that is up for debate in the Orthodox Church!"

How We Will Go about Reclaiming the Great Commission

From the start it is important to know that our way forward will not be found in debating the Divinity of Christ, nor will it be found in changing any of our Lord's teachings. It cannot be found in the dismantling of the Church, either. We are so incredibly fortunate to have inherited the full deposit of faith (Jude 1:3). As you will see, reclaiming the Great Commission is not about rejecting Church Tradition. Instead, this work is primarily a process of recovering and remembering who we are.

In the final verses of the Gospel of Matthew, Jesus tells His disciples, "Go . . . and make disciples of all the nations, baptizing them in the name of the Father and of the Son and of the Holy Spirit, teaching them to observe all things that I have commanded you" (Matt. 28:19–20). These were the last words Jesus said to His disciples before ascending into heaven. In time, this passage of Holy Scripture came to be known as the Great Commission. Jesus was reminding His disciples that He wanted everyone to hear and accept the teachings He had shared with them.

Looking back, we see that the apostles were faithful to Jesus' instructions. They set out to change the world with His message. Fortunately, this movement to spread the life of Jesus didn't end after the original band of twelve departed from this life. After them, others accepted Christ's commandment, and, sharing the same vision the Twelve Apostles had, new bands of followers also went forth as ambassadors of Christ.

Today as we survey the landscape within our Christian communities, we notice that many faithful followers of the Way (John 14:6) are still motivated by Jesus' life, His words, and His truth, and they too want to share the Good News with others.

Many examples remind us that evangelism and serving the Great Commission have always been a part of the life of the Church. We honor saints such as Nino of Georgia, who bears the title of Equal to the Apostles. She began her missionary work in the 300s. Saint Olga, from the 900s, also bears the title Equal to the Apostles. In more recent times, St. Herman of Alaska worked as an evangelist in the Kodiak Archipelago, spreading the gospel among the native population. This is a tiny selection of the thousands of missionaries and evangelists who kept the words of the Great Commission alive.

Unfortunately, many of us find ourselves hindered in some way in our ability to follow the words of the Great Commission. In facing this reality, some of us begin to wonder whether we are equipped to do this work, how to start, or where to look for answers. Others question whether the very vehicle for doing God's work—their local church—stands in the way, and they wonder how it can change. In some communities, the Great Commission has not motivated the actions of the members for decades; it has become a forgotten commandment of our Lord. Other parishes are simply trying to ensure their community's survival. In short, there are many reasons Christians are struggling with Christ's commission.

The purpose of this book is twofold. First, I hope to help us understand why some of us have lost our way. Second, I will discuss how we can get back on track and describe some ways to get there. We can take many simple and practical steps that will help us reclaim the

Great Commission. Along the way I will explore several foundational truths, or concepts, that I believe will deepen our understanding of what our communities can be.

We understand this process is both therapeutic and positive. In the Church we speak of the life and ministry of Christ as healing humanity from the disfigurement and illnesses of the Fall. He heals what is broken in us, which is therapeutic and remedial, but He also leads us into something positive beyond this: in Christ, we are given by grace a new inheritance that is greater than what we had in the Garden.

So also in reclaiming the Great Commission: we heal what is disfigured and broken in our parishes, but we also bring new elements to the life of the community, building it into something more than it ever was.

This process will require us to take a hard look at ourselves. In this we are following Jesus' first public words to fallen humanity: "Repent, for the kingdom of heaven is at hand!" (Matt. 3:2). To repent means to change our old way of thinking, to have a change of heart, and to begin to move and live in a new way.

This book may appear to be just another book on leadership or parish organization and management, but it is more than that. This book invites us to begin considering the Great Commission through the lens of our own personal repentance and transformation. In fact, this is one of the most important rules of this book: *Any change we hope to see in our communities has to occur first in ourselves.*

I hope this book will help not just your community but all of us to reclaim the Great Commission. Each individual and each community is important, and all our contributions are essential to the Body of Christ. So, whether you are part of a parish that has plateaued, a so-called dying community, or a new mission church, this book is for you. It is also designed for small groups, parish councils, and clergy. I believe every member in every community can benefit from reading and applying this material.

Finally, it may help to know what this book is not. It is not just a list of best practices or strictly a how-to guide. It is not only a workbook for leadership seminars—although it could be used as one—nor is it an academic treatment of leadership principles. Instead, we will be looking at the basics of parish health through the lens of the Faith Jesus entrusted to us and the tools He gives us by His grace and love.

May the promise of Christ encourage us in every step we take in reclaiming the Great Commission: "For where two or three are gathered together in My name, I am there in the midst of them" (Matt. 18:20).

How to Use This Book

A general note to the individuals and teams reading this book: At the end of each chapter, you will find a review divided into three sections: Main Ideas, Action Items, and For Contemplation. The Main Ideas section summarizes a few key points from the chapter. Action Items include a list of suggested steps you can take. The For Contemplation section contains prompts designed to help you think more deeply about the chapter topics.

Whether you are reading this book on your own or with others, I encourage you to keep a journal in which you can write down your thoughts and insights. If you are fortunate to be working through this book with a group, this journal will be useful for discussions about what you are reading. Keep in mind that this book is inviting you to change the way you view the Great Commission. And remember, any change we hope to see in our communities begins first in the transformation that occurs in each of us.

Admittedly, this book does not have all the answers you need to reclaim the Great Commission. However, it provides an opportunity for you to consider the steps you can take with others to prepare the soil of your hearts for new growth.

In the end, we cannot tackle this task alone. Not only do we need to seek the help of others, but we need to seek guidance from God. Too easily we can come up with a list of action items and thoughts without God, but this go-it-alone approach will impoverish our efforts. It is important to allow space for the Holy Spirit to work in our hearts and minds.

To help facilitate your connection with God, I suggest you spend some time in silence and prayer before journaling and discussing what you have read. For some additional thoughts on personal prayer, you can read my earlier book, *Toolkit for Spiritual Growth: A Practical Guide to Prayer, Fasting, and Almsgiving* (Ancient Faith Publishing, 2020). For now, before you reflect, journal, and share with others, I suggest that you begin by turning your attention and your heart toward God, seeking a closer connection with Jesus Christ. Spend some time sitting in silence, collecting yourself before the Lord. After quieting yourself, offer a prayer asking for His wisdom, illumination, and guidance.

I also want to encourage and remind you that God is already at work in your parish. He wants good things to occur, and He will work with you to bring them to fruition.

Review

Main Ideas

1. Our path forward is not found in debating the truths of our Faith. Rather, our journey lies in remembering and recovering who we are.

2. Each community is invited to respond to the Great Commission of Christ found in Matthew 28.

3. Responding to the Great Commission has become difficult for many of us. You are not alone.

4. Any change we hope to see in our communities must first occur in ourselves. Responding requires us to repent and change personally.

5. Health is our goal, not growth. Growth is a by-product of health.

Action Items

1. Form a group to read and discuss this book along with you.

2. Begin a journal of ideas gleaned from your reading.

3. Resolve to ask questions of yourself and others and to begin a dialogue.

For Contemplation

1. No one eats a salami in one sitting, but rather we eat one thin slice at a time. Biting off a little bit at a time will be important and ensure you do not become overwhelmed. Remember, Rome, as they say, was not built in a day.

2. Why is the first public word of Jesus "Repent"?

3. Not everything has to be done, nor do you have to do everything right, right away. Honestly, any little step your community takes is positive and helps you progress.

PART I

Lessons Learned
in Reclaiming
the Great Commission

CHAPTER ONE

The Story of Saint Spyridon Parish

Beginnings

YEARS AGO, I did something that some will say was foolish. In point of fact, several of my friends at the time told me that very thing. I had been a priest for approximately three years at a wonderful parish just outside Denver. I could easily have stayed there for the rest of my ministry and been quite comfortable. The parish was filled with friends and relatives with whom I had grown up, and it provided a welcoming home for my family.

But in the midst of this, I went to my bishop and did the unexpected. I told him I wanted to be transferred.

"What?" he asked. "Where do you want to go?"

I told him I didn't really know, but I wanted to start a mission parish.

"No," he replied in no uncertain terms.

Although his words were hard to hear at the time, I look back now and realize just how odd my request must have sounded. You see, part of the challenge we face from the outset of this journey toward reclaiming the Great Commission is our personal and collective amnesia. We have forgotten what a Christian community is and

21

what it could become. This forgetting of who we are is a barrier to the health of our parishes.

To put it another way, it is difficult for any of us to imagine a community that does not yet exist or does not fit our already-held notion of what a parish should be. My bishop couldn't make the leap. "What do you mean you want to start a *new* church?"

The truth is, our preconceived parameters of what a community *ought* to be often prevent us from seeing what it *could* be. This state of mind explains in part why my bishop responded immediately to my request without discussion. "You cannot start a mission parish," he said.

Of course, such thinking is problematic. Aren't we all supposed to respond to Christ's words in the Great Commission? Isn't this our mission?

Now, keep in mind that my request was not for a community split or a church plant—that is to say, the growth of one community out of another with the intent of becoming independent. Rather, what I was proposing was to start a Christian community from scratch and to do so in a place where no Orthodox parish had ever existed.

Even before I attended seminary, starting a mission parish was a secret dream of mine. It was an idea that had stirred in my heart and in my gut since I was a teenager, and one of the reasons was related to my experience of parish life. I started my life in the Church at a large cathedral parish. But at thirteen years old, I experienced a split—one that would lead to the forming of a new community.

This new parish had as one of its founding principles the idea of mission—or at least an openness to non-Christians. Prior to this experience, I had never met anyone in church who was not an Orthodox Christian. For that matter, I had never met anyone in church who was not *Greek* and Orthodox. As odd as this may sound, I would have been shocked if someone off the street had entered my childhood church. It just didn't happen.

I think this background is important, because had it not been for my experience with this new community, I probably could not have conceived of a parish that was established for the pure and simple reason of sharing the gospel of Jesus Christ and the Orthodox Faith with those who had never received either one. This new parish altered my understanding of what a church could be. I was a bit like the blind man who said, after the Lord restored his sight, "One thing I know: that though I was blind, now I see" (John 9:25).

Years later, I stood in the apartment of a seminary classmate and asked him a question. "What do you want to do after you graduate?"

He looked at me with a bit of confusion on his face. "Well, I want to be assigned to a parish and do my best to serve the people in it." Although I couldn't explain it at the time, his answer struck me as both admirable and narrow.

Thinking back to that exchange, I realize now how much the community split of my youth had influenced my understanding. Of course, my classmate's answer expressed a different view of church life, which was not necessarily better or worse than mine. But it may have been limiting. I should also say that our brief exchange could not have been a full explanation of how he felt about parish life or his vocational call. It was nothing more than a snapshot of his mindset at the time. Nevertheless, his words got me thinking. Was it my job after seminary simply to look after those who were already members of the parish I would be assigned to?

You see, I believe the thought of mission work should develop in the heart of every follower of Christ. The last words Jesus shared with His disciples before His glorious Ascension, the words now known as the Great Commission, are worth repeating here: "'Go therefore and make disciples of all the nations, baptizing them in the name of the Father and of the Son and of the Holy Spirit, teaching them to observe all things that I have commanded you; and lo, I am with you always, *even* to the end of the age.' Amen" (Matt. 28:19–20). For many years these words have stirred a fervent desire in me to share the gospel. In this I am in good company. The Apostle Paul felt the same way, and he wrote about his desire in 1 Corinthians 9:16: "For if I preach the gospel, I have nothing to boast of, for necessity is laid upon me; yes, woe is me if I do not preach the gospel!" For St. Paul and those who have experienced a similar calling, the words of Christ drive them beyond the familiar into uncharted territory.

A Dream Becomes a Reality

After a couple years of asking, including changes that could only have come about through God's providence, my bishop reluctantly agreed to my idea. I remember sitting in his office when he looked at me and said, "If you are sure you want to go, then you have two years, no more. Then I am transferring you right back to an established parish."

At the time he did not think this mission idea would work. How could it? He was going to send a priest to a town that had never had a full-time Orthodox priest. As I already mentioned, the idea of planting new Christian communities for people not already in the Church or accustomed to the gospel was hard for him to understand. It is worth repeating that the bishop's viewpoint, and to a degree my classmate's, are not unusual among Orthodox people.

I remember coming back to Denver a year or so into my time at my mission parish of Saint Spyridon and running into one of the Greek ladies who had watched me grow up in the cathedral parish of my youth. She was from the "old country," and at a social gathering after a service she approached me.

"Father, I never-a see you so long," she said with a smile and a heavy Greek accent. "Where-a you bin?" I explained to her that I was up north now in Loveland, Colorado. This news surprised her. "We gotta church there, lotta Greeks live-a up there?"

"No," I told her, "there aren't a lot of Greeks in northern Colorado." This news, I could see, confused her.

"Do the bishop know you up there now?"

"Yes." I assured her the bishop knew I was up there.

After thinking about it she responded, "Hmmm. Maybe he should-a close it."

Church planting for non-Orthodox people was not something many of us who grew up in an Orthodox parish could imagine. We were busy enough trying to take care of our own.

For many years, Orthodox Christians outside of traditional Orthodox countries arrived in new lands not as missionaries but as immigrants or refugees. These immigrants and refugees often came from countries where mission and outreach activities had been prohibited for centuries. There is not time or space in this short book to examine this history. Suffice it to say that most parishes in places like America, Canada, or Australia were established not to bring the gospel to new people but to provide Orthodox immigrants or new arrivals with a spiritual home. While this work of the Church was and is important, it is also possible that this model has created its own barriers.

These historical realities have led many communities and church leaders to live in a way that almost ignores Christ's final command. This may sound outrageous to some readers. How could the Great Commission be ignored? Let us who have experienced life differently not be too quick to judge, especially when we have benefited from living under different circumstances.

Today, it is important to see that a church that serves the needs of recent immigrants or its own members looks and acts very differently from a church focused on the Great Commission. Readjusting our focus is possible and does not require us to abandon our history. Rather, we can make small, constructive changes over time to meet the opportunities that face us and to move in a new direction.

Finding Balance

Even those who grew up with or have developed a good understanding of the Great Commission can benefit from this discussion. I have noticed that even missionaries experience a subtle but dangerous shift in their mindset over time. For example, at times I have become totally focused on those within the walls of my parish and forgotten those outside it. Within the first year of my time at Saint Spyridon, we received a major grant. After we received it, my first thought was about how this grant could stabilize our finances. I wanted to squirrel it away instead of using some of it to serve the community at large. My thoughts at that time were first about the safety of the parish and about self-preservation. I realized later how much of my thinking and focus had become inward. It is hard to direct our attention continually outward, but as we keep our sights on the Great Commission, this outward focus gets easier.

I do not mean we should fail to prioritize ministry to our own parishioners. In this I have also failed. I can become engrossed in sharing the gospel with those who have never heard of Christ and fail to continue to cultivate the faith of those who are attending each Sunday. One of the original members of the Saint Spyridon community pointed this out to me. He had noticed that I was spending more and more time with people who were exploring the Faith and less and less time with those who had already accepted Christ. This too was a narrow way of fulfilling my duties. Instead of this lopsided way of ministry, I have had to learn—and I am still learning—to balance the two by maintaining an effective and fervent ministry to our own people while also looking after the new people I encounter. In other words, I am learning that I need to do both!

There are lots of ways to examine how to maintain this balance. One practical way in which I evaluate myself is to look at how I spend my time. I also do this kind of evaluation with others in the parish; we review where we have placed our priorities as a community. We try to ask ourselves, *What ministries and activities are important to us, and whom do they serve?* In spending time with key members of my community on a regular basis and talking over this need for balance, I continue to learn how we can better reclaim the Great Commission.

Coming to Terms with My Other Limitations

Returning to my story, I have come to believe that even though my bishop couldn't envision a new community, he was nevertheless wise in other respects. For example, he knew just how ill prepared and inexperienced I was. In fact, I remember speaking to a dear friend around this time. He was a schoolteacher and the head of the math department at a large public high school. When I told him what I was up to, he was not exactly supportive. He explained to me that his school district understood the opening of a new school to be a very challenging endeavor—even a risky one. So many things could go wrong. As a result, the district had a policy of sending its most seasoned and experienced executive staff and teachers into new schools, making good use of the talents they had developed over many years of careful growth.

Unfortunately, this is not how most new Christian churches are formed. They are usually staffed by the youngest and least experienced among us, which is a bad idea. My first year in this new community was extremely rough, for many reasons. Simply put, I wasn't adequately prepared for what I faced, as my friend had suspected. Even though I had dreamed of starting a new parish established on the gospel and our Holy Tradition, and even though I went forth with joy and a great deal of exuberance, that was not enough. I felt lost and questioned myself.

It is important to note that at that time, a small but incredibly loving and eager group of Christians received me. In fact, this small group of six families had already begun to plant the seeds for a new church in the years before my arrival. Unconnected to my conversations with my bishop, they too had been speaking with him. They had asked that he send them a priest so that they could hold services once a month on a Sunday. (It is wonderful to see how God was working on them and me at the same time.) The bishop then asked a retired priest, Fr. Peter from nearby Cheyenne, Wyoming, to help this parish get started. Along with Fr. Peter, the members, out of their love for Christ and His Church, gave sacrificially of their time, talents, and treasure to form a new community.

This meant that as I left Denver, I wasn't exactly starting from scratch. Instead, some important groundwork had been laid, and the community of Saint Spyridon today will always be grateful for the initial vision and initiative of its founders. There is an obvious lesson to point out here: Reclaiming the Great Commission takes all of us. This task is not the effort of clergy, or laypeople, or even God alone. Rather, it is something God does along with all of us. Happily, we each have a part to play.

As fortunate as I was to step into this new community, their understanding of what to do and how to do it was, like mine, limited. My guess is that this limited understanding faces each of you, even in well-established Christian communities. In the years since the founding of Saint Spyridon, I have been blessed with the opportunity to tell my story in many places. Time and again, people have approached me and shared their delight in hearing that their experiences are mirrored in my own, even though our circumstances are different. Like me, they feel as if they have been wandering around without a clear picture of what to do. They are unsure how to share the gospel in a way that is transformative for them and those they meet.

In the beginning, I was unaware of the resources that would have helped me. (This is one of the main reasons I decided to write this book.) I also had not intentionally connected with mentors who could guide me. I didn't even know there were people who could help. Many years after I arrived at Saint Spyridon, a group of parishes in New England asked me to share my experiences. At the end of one of our sessions, a seventy-year-old council member in one of the local parishes exclaimed, "I have been serving on the council of my local church on and off for the last forty years, and this is the first time any-one has ever explained to me what I am supposed to be doing!"

Years later, I can say that this sentiment is widespread. People con-tinually contact me to ask, "What do I do?" They are not sure how to address their challenges or, more importantly, their opportunities.

Addressing these challenges and opportunities is the purpose of this book. And I guess it goes without saying, this is why you are reading it.

I didn't know how to build a newly formed parish. As far as I knew, only a few parishes existed like the one I was attempting to shepherd. In fact, at the time I knew of only one other parish that was similar to ours. That is not to say other communities didn't exist. The point is, I was not aware of them, and we were then not accustomed to helping one another in similar endeavors. This is true for existing communi-ties as well.

Again, as the years since Saint Spyridon's founding have rolled by, I have spoken to dozens of established Christian communities. Over and over, I hear how isolated and, to a degree, unsupported they feel. They are not aware of resources even within their own communities that can help, and, perhaps more importantly, they have not discussed their circumstances with others who are walking the same path. It is important therefore that we no longer sit passively waiting for help. Each of us should take initiative and responsibility for developing ourselves and our communities. Unquestionably, a positive way forward can be found, and the first step is within our power to take.

The way forward is especially difficult because reclaiming the Great Commission is not something seminarians and church leaders are trained to do. Mostly, I had been trained for a completely different paradigm—one that is quickly vanishing. The parish I was prepared and trained to serve does not really exist anymore. I think for many of us, the fantasy of that parish persists. We erroneously believe that a homogeneous church filled with spiritually connected and mature Christians, or even a society predisposed to the Christian story, still exists. We may think we are being sent into communities to manage the Christian experience and to administer the spiritual life of the faithful.

But our present reality is very different. The Christian story is increasingly unfamiliar in our culture. For example, not long ago, my neighbor's child noticed the cross I wore around my neck. This young boy looked up at me and asked, "Mr. Armatas, why are you wearing a plus sign around your neck?"

A simple online search will reveal to you that the group of unchurched in almost every place is growing faster than almost any religious segment of the population. More and more people under the age of thirty, when asked what faith tradition they are part of, identify themselves as "none."

Long after the founding of Saint Spyridon, I realized that in the early years I felt a bit like the two characters described in Tod Bolsinger's excellent book, *Canoeing the Mountains: Christian Leadership in Uncharted Territory*. He writes about Captain Meriwether Lewis and Second Lieutenant William Clark, who in the early 1800s were hired to explore the newly acquired western territory of the US.

Many people do not realize that these men were chosen for one main reason: they were watermen. They knew how to navigate rivers, so President Thomas Jefferson sent them to discover a water route that would connect the east and west coasts of this vast country.

But instead, Lewis and Clark found themselves climbing mountains—the Rocky Mountains—while dragging their canoes. They were forced to learn new skills, much as we are today. They were completely unaware of the terrain ahead of them when they set out on their journey, just as I was unprepared for the realities of establishing a new parish.

I was not the only one who recognized the immense challenge that lay before me. Some Sundays I would get home after Liturgy, and my wife would start to cry. "Why did you bring us here? What are we doing? I don't see how this is going to work."

Doubts began to creep into my mind as well, because as the months rolled by, everything was hard. It was hard because I didn't have a roadmap. It was hard because I was without proper training and experience. But the work was made all the more difficult because my pride was in the way.

Pride Plus Inexperience: A Deadly Combination

Pride was a major reason for my struggle. Pride, coupled with my lack of experience, made my situation all the more precarious. You see, I had made a number of assumptions about my abilities—about what I could and could not do, and about what I should do—based on my preconceived and limited notions of how things should be.

I could argue that no one should have expected more from me at the time. I could argue that we don't know what we don't know. For example, I couldn't have known what it meant to start a new community—or to transform and refashion an existing one—until I started, right? At least, I couldn't know without setting aside my pride and asking questions that would help me to step out of myself and what I take for granted.

What I lacked was humility. Humility leads us into meaningful dialogue with others and opens our minds about what needs to be done. I hadn't done much listening and engaging, so I remained ignorant and acted carelessly and thoughtlessly. These deficiencies of mine meant that my growth and the community's were stunted and more circuitous than they needed to be. Anyone starting out today would benefit greatly by not following my example. How easy it would have been to ask questions, seek help, and talk with those around me. This is something I hope readers of this book will in fact do.

It is worth repeating what I did have at this early stage: those few families and others who gathered to receive me as a new priest were exuberant and joyful. More importantly, they were ready for an adventure. To a degree, they had already unhitched themselves from some of the established—and somewhat restrictive—viewpoints of what it means to be an Orthodox parish in America. That openness was a huge asset, the value of which I did not fully grasp at the time.

So what happened? Things got moving slowly. At times we would have only a handful of people on Sunday; maybe only ten. Sometimes twenty or thirty would show up. But often we had few of the things we consider essential to conducting services. For example, there were times when I'd have no musicians to accompany the service, let alone staff or trained volunteers.

I remember with fondness one of my first liturgies. After opening it by proclaiming "Blessed is the Kingdom of the Father, and of the Son, and of the Holy Spirit," I was met by an uneasy silence. People were not sure of what to sing in response. In retrospect, I don't think that was their fault. As I mentioned earlier, they had already been gathering with Fr. Peter for Sunday services. However, my arrival, coupled with my inability to recognize what was already in place—a byproduct of my pride—meant that people got hurt and became uncertain and uncomfortable.

I wish I could go back in time and start again. Then I would be much more careful to assess and respect what I was stepping into. But, once again, I lacked humility. Instead, I learned the hard way how important it is to move slowly and thoughtfully when starting something new in a community.

In the silence on that Sunday, I had to stop the Liturgy, which is something I had never done before. But stop it is what I did, and right then and there we practiced singing the responses to the priest's petitions in the Divine Liturgy.

The Bishop Visits: Holy Unction

A little less than a year into my time at Saint Spyridon, my bishop called me in advance to tell me he was going to pay us a pastoral visit during the most important time of the liturgical calendar. He wanted to visit our parish on Wednesday of Holy Week.[1] For Orthodox Christians, Holy Week is the most complicated liturgical period of the year, and one of the sacraments of the Church, Holy Unction, is offered specifically on Wednesday. My bishop wanted to be present for and serve the parish at this sacrament, and frankly, I was nervous.

---

1   The Orthodox Church organizes time around a liturgical calendar. Even non-Christians in the West know something of this calendar. For example, most people are familiar with the Christian feasts of Christmas—more appropriately called the Nativity—which is celebrated on December 25, and Easter—more appropriately called Pascha—which is celebrated in the spring. In addition to these dates, the Church has laid out other events from the life of Christ that make up the liturgical year, such as Christ's Baptism, called Holy Theophany, on January 6, and the Transfiguration of Christ on August 6. Holy Week is one week of the liturgical year that follows a forty-day period known as Great Lent. In this week the Church remembers the last days of the life of Christ: the days of His entry into Jerusalem; His teachings there; His institution of the Eucharist; His betrayal; His arrest, trial, mocking, and scourging; His Crucifixion; and His Resurrection.

We had never celebrated all of Holy Week before. (In an Orthodox parish there are more than fifteen services prescribed for that week.) Who was going to come? Who would lead the singing and reading this complicated service required? Would those who came know how important and rare a visit from a bishop was?

The physical space we were in at the time was small, and it didn't fit many people—maybe sixty comfortably. Yet miraculously, when the bishop came, the room was full. There was only one problem: I didn't recognize many of the people who had come. As we went through the service, I realized that most of them were not Orthodox, and they were not familiar with our worship services. The little things clued me in: most of the newcomers didn't cross themselves[2] during our prayers, few kissed the icons in the narthex or lit a candle as they entered[3], and many looked as if they didn't know what was going on.

Those who had founded the parish were doing their best to accommodate our guests and share with them as much as they could about what to do in the service. There we were in the middle of the unction service[4], and I was feeling lost, as if I were climbing a mountain while holding a paddle and lugging a canoe. What do you do when you figure out that most of the people in your church service are not Orthodox Christians?

I leaned over to the bishop and whispered, "I think we have to have two lines—one for the Orthodox and one for the non-Orthodox."

---

2   Crossing ourselves is a physical action Orthodox often make in worship. We trace the sign of the cross over ourselves, using our right hand, starting at the forehead then proceeding down to the chest/heart, then over to the right shoulder and ending on the left. It is an act of prayer and piety that recalls the saving power of Christ and His death upon the Cross.

3   It is customary for Orthodox Christians upon entering the church to light a candle, thus receiving the light of Christ into their lives, and to venerate (kiss) the icon of our Lord.

4   In the Sacrament of Holy Unction the Church remembers the ill effects of sin and the need for healing from its disfigurement and from the sicknesses of the flesh.

(The holy unction is reserved for Orthodox Christians.)

He looked at me quizzically and whispered back, "What did you just say?"

I repeated myself, only this time a little louder. "We have to have two lines. One for the Orthodox and one for the non-Orthodox."

He replied, "What are you going to do with the non-Orthodox, Father Evan?"

Honestly, when I opened my mouth I was not sure, so I blurted out the first thing that came to my mind. "Anoint them using the oil from the altar vigil lamp?"[5]

At the end of the unction service, we announced that we would be anointing people and that there would be two lines. I asked the Orthodox Christians to please line up in front of our bishop, and he would anoint them with holy unction. Those who were not Orthodox were to come to my line, and I would anoint them with oil from the vigil lamp on the altar.

Guess whose line was longer?

My bishop anointed a few people, and I anointed a few dozen.

What I Learned from That Visit

Even today there are not that many Orthodox Christians in Loveland, Colorado, but at that time, there were even fewer. This was an important lesson for us, just as it should be for you. If we hope to share our Faith, we need to understand that we are offering something unknown to almost everyone we will meet and that the way to share it is not clearly marked. This means that although who we are and what we teach are not up for debate, we should be willing to adapt to our surroundings and change what we can. Such adaptation requires

---

5   An oil lamp is kept on the altar table of an Orthodox church. This oil lamp
     typically remains lit throughout the year to remind us of the unwaning light of
     Christ.

us to be humble, flexible without compromise, and clear about our core values. It also requires us to ask questions we may not have asked before and to discern what change looks like without changing the unchangeable. In such a state, we learn to respond peacefully and intentionally instead of reacting negatively or even dismissively to the unexpected circumstances we encounter.

One example of this adaptability is our response when non-Christians ask us to hold a prayer service (memorial) for their loved ones who have died. This happened recently when a large family in our town who were not Orthodox lost a child and turned to our parish for prayer. We ended up hosting over thirty people on a Sunday after Liturgy for that prayer service.

What about the man who asked me if I could hear his confession even though he was not a member of the Church? I decided that nothing prohibited me from listening and praying with him. This is now something I do regularly with people who are not yet a part of our parish.

How do we respond to those inside the church who wonder about the melodies of the hymns we sing and ask if we can try singing them differently? This is a much trickier conversation. Or how do we accommodate people during our worship services who are not Christian? Then there are the questions about which ministries get priority and funding and why certain activities are left undone.

What I have noticed is that time and again, as I experience new things, I am challenged. At times I get scared, and I think about pulling back and abandoning the hard work of reclaiming the Great Commission. At other times I long for the familiar patterns of my youth, when everyone around me came from a similar background. Often I am tempted to react with anger because people either act or see things differently than I do. I can resent the fact that they fail to see my vision. I can easily get stuck in my version of how parish life should be, and I can't see what is possible. Others in my community may react in the same way.

As I think again and again about that first unction service, I am reminded of what it taught me. It is important to be open to my surroundings and to consider thoughtfully a response that does not set aside who we are but also does not ignore what we face.

To be honest, it can be easier to ignore the tensions our new surroundings present to us, but reclaiming the Great Commission requires us to pay attention to them and respond. I think one simple step we can take in this direction is to assess our experiences thoughtfully, to examine the things we may be ignoring or feeling in our communities, and to begin a conversation about them with one another. I am not saying the answers will come easily—they didn't with the issue of the music in our parish. But the answers certainly will not come if we avoid talking about them. Throughout this book and in the final chapter specifically, I will offer more ideas about how to move forward in a positive way. For now, let me say we should at least plan to talk, to think, and to talk some more so that we can respond intentionally and graciously to our experiences.

Synergy

That experience during the unction service affected me in a profound way. In the years since, as I have shared this story, people have often asked, "How did the people who came find out about the service?" Or "Why did they come?" Or, more commonly, "Did you advertise on radio or in the paper to draw people to the service that evening?" We did nothing to publicize the service. I have come to understand that a combination of things led people to show up at Saint Spyridon that day.

Our Orthodox Faith teaches us that God and human beings work together for the salvation of the world. This theological concept is known in the Church as *synergia*. In no way does this mean that God's plan of salvation or His redeeming work is somehow imperfect or limited. Rather, the theological concept of synergy reminds us of our part—a part God has given to us. We should think here about the Archangel Gabriel's visit to a young woman named Mary as a primary example of synergy. Clearly stated, God's plan included Mary's participation.

> Now in the sixth month the angel Gabriel was sent by God to a city of Galilee named Nazareth, to a virgin betrothed to a man whose name was Joseph, of the house of David. The virgin's name *was* Mary. And having come in, the angel said to her, "Rejoice, highly favored *one*, the Lord *is* with you; blessed *are* you among women!" But when she saw him, she was troubled at his saying, and considered what manner of greeting this was. Then the angel said to her, "Do not be afraid, Mary, for you have found favor with God. And behold, you will conceive in your womb and bring forth a Son, and shall call His name JESUS. He will be great, and will be called the Son of the Highest; and the Lord God will give Him the throne of His father David. And He will reign over the house of Jacob forever, and of His kingdom there will be no end." Then Mary said to the angel, "How can this be, since I do not know a man?" And the angel answered and said to her, "*The* Holy Spirit will come upon you, and the power of the Highest will overshadow you; therefore, also, that Holy One who is to be born will be called the Son of God. Now indeed, Elizabeth your relative has also conceived a son in her old age; and this is now the sixth month for her who was called barren. For with God nothing will be impossible." Then Mary said, "Behold the maidservant of the Lord! Let it be

to me according to your word." And the angel departed from her. (Luke 1:26–38)

Yes, Jesus' Incarnation was God's plan, but Mary agreed to participate. Her decision was not only important—it was decisive. She decided to work with God to bring about the Birth of our Savior.

Trusting God and Developing Ourselves

In the years since that memorable service, people have continued to show up at Saint Spyridon, seemingly out of nowhere. It is not unusual for us to welcome guests at almost every service. (I say "guest" because I feel the word "visitor" implies a wrong attitude. A visitor is someone we don't expect to see again.) And even though in the years since that first Holy Week we have established a larger footprint in our town through our involvement in it, the fact remains that our ability to reclaim the Great Commission continues to be a synergistic act. On the one hand we recognize that "every good gift and every perfect gift is from above, and comes down from the Father of lights" (James 1:17), but we also need to do our part.

I often encourage other parishes who have not yet experienced regular visits from guests by reminding them that my situation is not different from theirs. Loveland, Colorado, does not have some special connection to the Holy Spirit. Moreover, our parish is not made up of highly trained specialists in church health and growth. Rather, we have come to recognize that in every place, no matter its size or context, God is moving and working. He has endowed people with gifts that can be cultivated and deployed.

The constant that should comfort us in our work of reclaiming the Great Commission is this: God loves us, knows us, and is working alongside us to bring everyone into His Church. Think about the history of God's interaction with people. Time and again we see His

Spirit at work, drawing all people to Himself. At the same time, one of the main premises of this book is that we must recognize that if our parishes lack vitality and growth, the fault is with us. Recall Jesus' parable of the banquet:

> A certain man gave a great supper and invited many, and sent his servant at supper time to say to those who were invited, "Come, for all things are now ready." But they all with one *accord* began to make excuses. The first said to him, "I have bought a piece of ground, and I must go see it. I ask you to have me excused." And another said, "I have bought five yoke of oxen, and I am going to test them. I ask you to have me excused." Still another said, "I have married a wife, and therefore I cannot come." So that servant came and reported these things to his master. Then the master of the house, being angry, said to his servant, "Go out quickly into the streets and lanes of the city, and bring in here *the* poor and *the* maimed and *the* lame and *the* blind." And the servant said, "Master, it is done as you commanded, and still there is room." Then the master said to the servant, "Go out into the highways and hedges, and compel *them* to come in, that my house may be filled." (Luke 14:16–23)

In this story, the man who sends out supper invitations is the Lord. Sadly, while many are invited, they all make excuses for not attending. In a parish setting, we understand the parable working out in the following way: The master's invitation to attend the banquet represents God's constant love and activity on behalf of our community. Yet while the Lord is working tirelessly to bring people to Himself, some of us have made excuses or built barriers. These barriers, which we will discuss later, don't stop God from continuing to draw all people to Himself (John 12:32), but they do hinder what can occur in our community. This is an important concept for us. We need to identify and remove these barriers and excuses if we hope to reclaim the Great Commission.

This, however, is not all we must do. When the Sacrament of Holy Baptism is celebrated, it begins at the back of the church, in the narthex. There we read through a series of prayers that recall our estrangement from God and the influence evil can have in our lives, leading us away from communion with God. This part of the service culminates with us standing outside the church, renouncing Satan. Interestingly, this is only a small part of the service. The rest of the sacrament is a movement toward God. After renouncing Satan, we walk back into the church and, in a sense, toward God, and our prayer takes on a more positive tone.

At this point we are no longer considering what we have failed to do and the things we must strip away. Instead, we are invited to consider what positive actions we can take—what we can add. This part of the service begins with a series of affirmations.

It is easy to relate this part of the baptismal service to reclaiming the Great Commission. As we mentioned above, our work will involve identifying and removing barriers and excuses. But it must also be focused on the positive steps we need to take. We should take initiative and use the intellect and talents God has given us (Matt. 25:14–30) to affect the health of our community. Note the simple fact that while the master gives the servant an order to fill his house with guests, the servant does not respond as some mindless lackey carrying out orders, nor does he refuse to participate. Rather, together the master and the servant seek out people who will accept the invitation to attend the banquet.

Looks Like You'd Better Stay

A year after that Holy Week service, the bishop returned for another pastoral visit. After a Sunday Liturgy in which the church was almost full, he turned to me and said, "Looks like you'd better stay." In just a short time, a noticeable transformation had occurred, and something special was beginning to happen. What had begun with a congregation often numbering in the single digits was already beginning to outgrow its small church building.

The growth and outreach Saint Spyridon has experienced is not, and should not be, an anomaly. In the following chapters we will look at key concepts and steps that will help you join in this process of reclaiming the Great Commission.

Review[6]

Main Ideas

1. The Great Commission is our mission, no matter the setting.

2. Identifying barriers based on past decisions is an important first step.

3. We need to maintain a balance between looking inward at our own members and looking outward at the potential for growth.

4. Moving forward is a synergistic act between God and human beings. We should rejoice in God's constant attention to our community's well-being without failing to do our work.

5. God is working and moving in your community.

---

6   Don't forget the recommendations I gave in the Introduction on how to move through your review.

Action Items

1. Discuss chapter 1 with the group you formed after reading the Introduction.

2. In the journal you started, write down some of the action items you discovered in this chapter.

3. Talk through the main points of the chapter listed above. See if you can refrain from reaching any quick conclusions but instead focus on developing questions and dialogue.

4. Review your personal and community calendar to determine where you spend your time and what that tells you about your parish's priorities.

5. Resolve from this point forward to ask questions of yourself and others and to begin a dialogue. Focus on dialogue, listening, and asking good questions.

For Contemplation

1. Does the Great Commission guide your decisions?

2. What can you change without changing the unchangeable?

3. What does synergy look like in your parish?

4. What assumptions do you have about your community? What are you taking for granted? What questions are you not asking?

5. How has your pride and inexperience limited your development?

6. Walk through your church as if you were visiting it for the first time. Think of every step and detail from the perspective of someone new. Look carefully at your campus, the buildings, and the grounds as if for the first time. What would you change? Do this again, but this time do it during a Sunday Liturgy. Arrive at church and pay attention to how you are greeted, what the experience of walking into the church during the service is like, and what you notice during the Liturgy and afterward. If you have a

fellowship time after the service, what is this experience like for someone new? Or consider asking someone you know to visit and observe, and get their feedback on the experience.

CHAPTER TWO

Five Essentials

Things We Do, Things We Fail to Do

WHEN I WAS TWELVE YEARS OLD, my mother packed me off to a summer church camp just outside of Laramie, Wyoming. Many things occurred that week that have stayed with me all my life. One of them was preparing for and giving my first confession to Fr. Dean, a priest who had a profound impact on my life. Because I had never given a confession before, I asked him to help me prepare. He gave me a prayer book that I still use today. In it was a preparation for confession that he authored. As I prepared, I remember coming across the idea that my sins were not just things I had done but also things I had failed to do. This concept was a revelation.

In the Introduction to this book, I shared the story of meeting a former Episcopal priest, Fr. Elias. That experience has also stayed with me over the years, and it planted a seed for understanding what it means to reclaim the Great Commission. Specifically, enabling a parish to thrive and grow does not hinge on quibbling over the theological norms of the Orthodox Church. Rather, as we discussed briefly in chapter 1, enabling a parish to thrive requires two things:

» eliminating the barriers that prevent us from living the time-less truths of our Faith, and

» discovering what needs to be done, as well as the things we have failed to do.

Thankfully, barriers are often hidden in plain sight, which means we don't have to look very far. Moreover, they are not found in what we would describe as our Holy Apostolic Tradition, as the story of Fr. Elias illustrates. These barriers are sometimes simple, seemingly innocuous customs, behaviors, and oversights. They may also be complex and deeply ingrained routines and ways of thought that must be rooted out and discarded, such as making people feel unwelcome or failing to develop leaders within our community.

At the same time, there is another side to reclaiming the Great Commission that I learned during my first confession: all the things I need to do but have not done. These are opportunities for change and new ways of thinking. These opportunities can be straightforward or complicated, as the following story illustrates.

The Space Shuttle Challenger *and the Little Things*

In 1985 I began my tenth-grade year at Overland High School in Aurora, Colorado. On January 28, 1986, as we started our second semester, the entire school filled the gym for an assembly. We were there to watch the launch of the space shuttle *Challenger*. Seventy-three seconds into its flight, the twenty-fifth shuttle mission ended in disaster. Mission control responded to the disintegration of the shuttle with understatement: "Obviously a major malfunction." We watched the loss of life in silent horror.

After a lengthy and in-depth review, investigators determined that a relatively small and inexpensive part caused one of our nation's most tragic space program disasters: the now-infamous O-ring.

The irony of this terrible event was that one of the most complex pieces of machinery ever developed by human beings up to that point—something that could literally take humans from Earth into the heavens and back again—was destroyed by something as simple as a gasket.

Regrettably, another more complex reason caused the *Challenger* to come apart. We eventually learned that several top engineers within NASA had sounded the alarm about the O-ring long before the shuttle's fatal flight. The entire disaster and loss of life could have been avoided! Unfortunately, no one within NASA took serious note of the engineers' warnings that a catastrophe was looming. Along with a breakdown in personal initiative and responsibility at all levels, the leadership at NASA failed to act.

In parish life, we often see similar dynamics at work. Our critical failure point is not, for example, our theology, our worship, or our Holy Tradition. Instead, the small things tend to take us apart, such as ignoring guests who visit our communities. The inaction of parish leadership, as in the NASA example, can become a critical failure point as well. A more complicated example of this type of neglect is our failure to develop ourselves and others as leaders within our parishes. (See the discussion on leadership in chapter 6.)

The questions I have been asking myself are: What keeps us from eliminating the barriers that stand in the way of our parish's health? How can we identify problem areas, both simple and complex, and learn to do what is best for our community?

Five Essentials on Our Journey

In the next few pages, I hope to answer these questions by talking about five essential concepts. I believe these can help us avoid the kinds of failures that led to the *Challenger* disaster.

1. Regaining our sight

2. Remembering our life-saving mission

3. Pruning

4. Building bridges, not barriers

5. Developing a sense of urgency

Regaining Our Sight

A candle stand is often the first thing you see when you enter an Orthodox church. There people light candles, reminding us that we come to the church to receive the light of Christ (John 1:3–4). The candles also remind us that we are to participate in spreading this light.

My whole life, I have entered church and lit a candle. However, when I arrived at Saint Spyridon, something about this familiar action bothered me. Like almost every parish I had ever visited, Saint Spyridon placed the candle stand in the entry of the church. And as in every other parish I had ever visited, an usher stood behind it.

In most places the candle stand is also a place where people pick up printed materials and leave an offering. This type of arrangement is familiar to those who have grown up in the Church. However, if this is your first time entering an Orthodox parish, the whole setup might strike you as unusual and even a bit intimidating. I realized this for the first time when I entered Saint Spyridon.

With the candle stand positioned away from the wall and someone standing behind it, the area felt more like a business counter than a sacred space. When guests walked inside the church, they immediately experienced someone watching them, standing behind what might appear to be a transaction counter. What is a newcomer supposed to do? Register somewhere? Pay for an admission ticket?

So I did something about this. I pushed the candle stand against the wall and asked the ushers to greet people while standing to the side of it. This is a small change—simply rearranging furniture—but now the first thing a guest encounters on entering Saint Spyridon is a friendly face, not a big wooden barrier.

I learned about the importance of viewing the familiar with fresh eyes when I went to business school in the 1980s at Boston College. I remember a case study on McDonald's that examined one of their corporate training tools. McDonald's moved new corporate employees from one location to another during their training. The professor asked us, "Why would McDonald's do this with new employees?"

The answer was simple but profound. McDonald's corporate leaders believed that a new manager in a new location could see things that an established manager, because of over-familiarity with his or her own restaurant, could not. These new trainees were learning an important lesson: We can become blind without even realizing it.

Growing up in my dad's diner, I had learned the same thing: how to walk into the restaurant and notice trash in the parking lot, fingerprints on the glass of the front door, or impatient customers in the lobby who hadn't been helped. I didn't realize it at the time, but my dad was helping me to see what needed to be seen.

This is not a new concept. In fact, I learned that C. S. Lewis wrote The Chronicles of Narnia as an attempt to reintroduce Christ to a society that he felt had grown overly accustomed to Him. By placing his readers in a new setting, Lewis gave them new eyes. Through the character of Aslan we can appreciate, as if for the first time, the beauty and wonder of meeting our Savior.

Regaining our sight in our parishes requires a similar approach: we need to see things anew. We need to develop a fresh perspective on the life of our community. This occurs when we develop what could be labeled a questioning attitude. In this mindset we make careful observations, consider what we see through our experiences and what is happening around us, and explore new ideas and options.

This mindset should be contrasted with that of doing things the way we've always done them simply because we tend to fall in line with our established traditions. Regaining our sight encourages us to be curious and to view curiosity and questions as positive. Regaining our sight does not mean we throw everything out. Instead, it allows us to observe things carefully and a bit critically. A mentor of mine has pointed out that this recapturing of vision is the first 10 percent of what needs to be done. The other 90 percent is the actions we take based on what we see.

This process of regaining our sight is also like the recovery of sight the blind man experienced in John 9.

> [Jesus] spat on the ground and made clay with the saliva; and He anointed the eyes of the blind man with the clay. And He said to him, "Go, wash in the pool of Siloam" (which is translated, Sent). So he went and washed, and came back seeing. (vv. 6–7)

The man's ability to see was not restored all at once. The man, who had been born blind, had his physical sight restored once he went to the pool of Siloam and washed. However, it took some time for him to truly see who Jesus was. We learn as we read that the man first understands Jesus as just another man—"A Man called Jesus" (v. 11), then as "a prophet" (v. 17). Finally, as the story closes, he worships Jesus as his Lord and God (v. 38).

Interestingly, as the story unfolds, we also read about the opposition the man faces. The community around him, which includes the religious leaders and even his parents, is not only skeptical but hostile. They question him again and again and even argue that what has happened is the result of Jesus' being a sinner. They refuse to see.

This same process plays out when we step into the holy task of healing our communities. While our sight is slowly restored over time, people who are important to us may not only resist the good we are doing but even call it evil. Amazingly, the blind man courageously stands up to those who oppose him, despite their threats and willful blindness. His response is our example in the process of change. (We will delve more deeply into the problem of resistance in chapter 5.)

Interestingly, the process of regaining our sight never ends. Rather, it becomes an ongoing essential in our journey toward reclaiming the Great Commission. This is not easily accomplished. It is easy to fall again into a state of blindness.

For instance, many Orthodox worship and liturgical practices are hard to understand and follow. This is true for those who grew up in an Orthodox parish but even more so for those who did not. As I regained my sight, I began to see difficulties from a guest's perspective. In response, I began explaining the most basic as well as the most complex aspects of our worship. In time, we developed service books that contained every prayer, hymn, and movement as well as directed instruction on liturgical worship so that people could follow things more easily.

We can find another example of regaining our sight in the area of ministry. Fortunately, almost every Greek Orthodox parish has an organization called Philoptochos. Yet most people do not know what the word means. It is a compound word that comes from the Greek words for "love" and "the poor." When combined, it means "love of the poor." By using the phrase "love of the poor" in conjunction with the word *Philoptochos*, I was able to help our community regain their vision for what this ministry is about and what its main objectives are.

When we commit ourselves to continually regaining our sight, this commitment facilitates our renewal, leading to a healthier parish. I have come to realize that regaining my sight means I can never go on autopilot. Parish life is too dynamic, and whenever I attempt to sit still or coast, I get into trouble. Just when I think I understand my surroundings, I have to begin again.

This was never truer than in March of 2020. Just as Saint Spyridon began its annual pilgrimage through Great Lent, a worldwide pandemic led to the closure of the parish. COVID-19 meant we had to reimagine what it meant to be a church. We had to close the parish and reopen it in a different way. Doing this required me to see things in a new way. It required regaining my sight.

Remembering Our Lifesaving Mission

In 1953 the Rev. Dr. Theodore Wedel of the Episcopal Church wrote a modern-day parable that has circulated widely on the internet. It is insightful on many levels:

> On a dangerous seacoast where shipwrecks often occur, there was once a crude little lifesaving station. The building was just a hut, and there was only one boat, but the few devoted members kept a constant watch over the sea, and with no thought for themselves, they went out day or night, tirelessly searching for the lost. Many lives were saved by this wonderful little station, so that it became famous. Some of those who were saved, and various others in the surrounding areas, wanted to become associated with the station and give of their time and money and effort for the support of its work. New boats were bought, and new crews were trained. The little lifesaving station grew.
>
> Some of the new members of the station were unhappy that the building was so crude and so poorly equipped. They felt that a more comfortable place should be provided as the first refuge of those saved from the sea. So they replaced the emergency cots with beds and put better furniture in an enlarged building.

Now the lifesaving station became a popular gathering place for its members, and they redecorated it beautifully and furnished it as a sort of club. Fewer of the members were now interested in going to sea on lifesaving missions, so they hired lifeboat crews to do this work. The mission of lifesaving was still given lip service, but most were too busy or lacked the necessary commitment to take part in the lifesaving activities personally.

About this time a large ship was wrecked off the coast, and the hired crews brought in boatloads of cold, wet, and half-drowned people. They were dirty and sick, and some of them had black skin, and some spoke a strange language, and the beautiful new club was considerably messed up. So the property committee immediately had a shower house built outside the club where victims of shipwrecks could be cleaned up before coming inside.

At the next meeting, there was a split in the club membership. Most of the members wanted to stop the club's lifesaving activities as being unpleasant and a hindrance to the normal life pattern of the club. But some members insisted that lifesaving was their primary purpose and pointed out that they were still called a lifesaving station. They were finally voted down and told that if they wanted to save the lives of all the various kinds of people who were shipwrecked in those waters, they could begin their own lifesaving station down the coast.

They did. As the years went by, the new station experienced the same changes that had occurred in the old. They evolved into a club, and yet another lifesaving station was founded. If you visit the seacoast today, you will find a number of exclusive clubs along that shore. Shipwrecks are still frequent in those waters, only now most of the people drown.

I once did a search on the internet and came across a photograph that showed what Rev. Wedel described: a lifesaving station that had been converted into a banquet facility. I show this image to leaders when I talk to them about reclaiming the Great Commission. It powerfully represents a position many of us find ourselves in today.

Stephen Covey, in his famous work *The Seven Habits of Highly Effective People,* coined the phrase, "The main thing is to keep the main thing the main thing." Often in our communities, the main thing is no longer the main thing, as Rev. Wedel's parable illustrates. It is important to note how insidiously the peripheral—the unimportant—comes to occupy the center of our attention and efforts.

Once at church camp, I illustrated the importance of setting priorities by using a bunch of rocks. On a table I had placed a large, clear container. Next to it were two piles—one of fist-sized rocks and the other of pebbles. The big rocks had important words written on them like "love," "mercy," and "forgiveness." A sign in front of the pile of pebbles said, "Everything else." I told everyone that the goal of the exercise was to place *all* the rocks into the container. I then asked for a volunteer to come forward to attempt to get the rocks, big and small, to fit into the container. The volunteer failed.

The solution, as I then demonstrated, was simple. The big rocks must be placed first, followed by the pebbles. If you put the small rocks in first, or even if you try to layer them in, the big ones will not fit into the container. The same is true in setting our priorities as a community. The big and essential things must come first, or the small things will crowd them out. Often this occurs without our noticing.

To counter this deadly disease, we must keep a constant remembrance of the lifesaving mission God has entrusted to us. Leaders who think in this way work hard every day at pushing the unimportant to the side so they can focus on the essential. The apostles faced this same challenge, and we read about it in Acts 6:1–7:

Now in those days, when *the number of* the disciples was mul-
tiplying, there arose a complaint against the Hebrews by the
Hellenists, because their widows were neglected in the daily
distribution. Then the twelve summoned the multitude of the
disciples and said, "It is not desirable that we should leave the
word of God and serve tables. Therefore, brethren, seek out
from among you seven men of *good* reputation, full of the Holy
Spirit and wisdom, whom we may appoint over this business;
but we will give ourselves continually to prayer and to the ministry of the word."

And the saying pleased the whole multitude. And they chose
Stephen, a man full of faith and the Holy Spirit, and Philip, Pro-
chorus, Nicanor, Timon, Parmenas, and Nicolas, a proselyte
from Antioch, whom they set before the apostles; and when
they had prayed, they laid hands on them.

Then the word of God spread, and the number of the disciples multiplied greatly in Jerusalem, and a great many of the
priests were obedient to the faith.

The apostles too found that their focus and their time were easily
gobbled up by tasks that were not central to their mission.

In the history of the Church, many faithful Christians refused
to lose sight of the lifesaving mission. These saints were unyielding
when it came to setting priorities and keeping their focus. In fact,
the Church reveres entire categories of saints for their ability to stay
locked on the mission of lifesaving. Two types of these saints are
anchorites and stylites. Anchorites are Christians whose singular
focus on Christ and the gospel caused them to leave secular society
and live in a small cell, sometimes literally walling themselves in to
ensure that they kept their priorities straight. Stylites did something
similar. They cut themselves off from distractions by choosing to

live on the top of a pillar, opting for a life that kept them constantly focused on Christ.

The well-known story of St. Moses the Ethiopian is retold in *The Sayings of the Desert Fathers* by Benedicta Ward:

A brother at Scetis committed a fault. A council was called to which Abba Moses was invited, but he refused to go to it. Then the priest sent someone to say to him, "Come, for everyone is waiting for you." So he got up and went. He took a leaking jug, filled it with water, and carried it with him. The others came out to meet him, seeing the trail of water behind him, and said, "What is this, Father?" The old man said to them, "My sins run out behind me, and I do not see them, and today I am coming to judge the errors of another." When they heard that, they said no more to the brother but forgave him.[7]

Saint Moses was unwilling to lose his focus and thus lose the message of the gospel, so he went to great, although unusual, lengths to ensure he remembered the lifesaving mission of the Church: "For the Son of Man has come to seek and to save that which was lost" (Luke 19:10). Jesus' words remind us that He was on a lifesaving mission. I've lost count of the number of times I have been encouraged to take up a different mission, but this verse reminds me of our purpose here on earth. As the parable of the lifesaving station points out, we must focus on our mission.

During my first two years at Saint Spyridon, I—along with many others—spent hundreds of hours developing a Greek festival. It quickly became lucrative and popular, but by the third year the

---

7   Ward, Benedicta, and Metropolitan Anthony. *The Sayings of the Desert Fathers: The Alphabetical Collection*, Vol. 59 (Collegeville, MN: Liturgical Press, 1984), 138–139.

festival was gone. Its dissolution, while painful, was the right move. You see, the planning and running of the festival had overtaken our lifesaving mission. In those early years it became the largest endeavor of our community. It started to suck up all our volunteer hours, our attention, and our focus. It had to go, because reclaiming the Great Commission hinges on remembering our lifesaving mission and refusing to deviate from it.

In my travels around the United States, I have met leaders from other parishes who have faced similar challenges. I remember one community that completely retooled its annual festival and turned it into a Festival of Orthodoxy instead of a Greek festival. The point of doing so was to reorient themselves toward the Great Commission.

Pruning

The decision to shut down our festival is an example of pruning and its importance. Without pruning—trimming back the nonessential—the task of staying focused becomes increasingly difficult. My mother taught me this lesson through her rose garden.

While growing up, I liked tending the roses each summer. To this day I love the fragrance of roses. However, pruning them was not something I enjoyed. Rose bushes have thorns, and no matter how careful I was, those thorns pricked me when I touched them.

I also resisted removing a rose blossom that had not yet died but was fading. I wanted to let the roses stay on the bush, but my mother would encourage me to prune them. She taught me that a fading rose that was left to wither and die on the stem would strip the bush of its vitality. It sucked away resources that the new buds and blooms needed.

In a sense, the festival was doing exactly that—it was taking away needed resources from the rest of the parish. As we all know, our resources are limited. There are only so many hours in each day, and as the illustration about rocks in the previous section makes clear, we have to set our priorities. Our festival sucked up so many limited and precious hours and resources that other, more essential tasks became almost impossible to attempt, let alone complete.

Reshaping where we spend our time is a form of pruning. It frees up hours and resources to be redirected toward the essential task of reclaiming the Great Commission.

The same holds true for many traditions in our communities. We often fail to prune what is dying or draining the life from us. We know from experience that if we make a tough decision, we will get pricked. This is painful, so we may hesitate to act. We also have difficulty with cutting an event that we have worked so hard in the past to cultivate. Yet a failure to prune leads to a weakening of the whole parish, especially when the thing that needs pruning isn't central to reclaiming the Great Commission.

Another way to look at pruning is to compare it to getting in shape physically. Let us suppose that you started going to the gym and working out. At the same time, despite your new commitment to physical exercise, you continued smoking, drinking excessively, and eating poorly. Your workouts likely would not have their desired effect, because your bad habits would be undermining your good ones. The same is true in the parish setting. If we want to reclaim the Great Commission, we need to take a good look at any barriers that are keeping us from fulfilling our purpose, and we need to prune. Doing this often makes room for what we should be doing, as the Scriptures show us.

Jesus said, "I am the true vine, and My Father is the vinedresser. Every branch in Me that does not bear fruit, He takes away; and every *branch* that bears fruit He prunes, that it may bear more fruit" (John 15:1–2). Pruning in this passage is a positive action that leads to fruitfulness. When we prune, we are actually setting our community up for new growth.

Building Bridges, Not Barriers

Bridges make it possible for people to cross over an obstacle. In effect, a bridge removes the obstacle. A bridge is open and is not selective. Anyone may cross it, because the bridge's job is to facilitate the free and easy movement of people. In a sense, a bridge is an invitation to engage.

In the 1800s, Ivan Kasatkin was born in Russia. He was later ordained to the priesthood as Fr. Nicholas. As a young man he traveled to Japan. His departure allowed him to follow his heart's desire to live as a missionary and heed Christ's commandment of the Great Commission. An intense period of studying Japanese language, culture, religion, and customs made it possible for him to bridge what initially appeared to be insurmountable barriers to spreading the gospel.

Thankfully, St. Nicholas of Japan was determined not to allow the barriers that stood in his way to keep him from developing a vibrant and growing community. The barriers he faced were many. From the start, he struggled to learn Japanese. He was unable to find coworkers and fellow missionaries, and he was met by hostility and opposition from the local population at almost every turn.

Additionally, the small Russian Orthodox community in Japan was not interested in engaging with the local population. Instead, the church had been concerned up to that time with serving its own people and retaining its distinctively Russian customs, traditions, and language. When St. Nicholas arrived in Japan, services were still being held only in Church Slavonic.

By the time St. Nicholas fell asleep in the Lord, the Church in Japan had grown exponentially. From one small chapel on the grounds of the Russian consulate, in 50 years St. Nicholas had established 266 communities.

Sadly, some parish communities are not in the business of building bridges. Instead they focus on barriers. Rather than welcoming and engaging all kinds of people, they become selective.

In one of His parables, Jesus says, "The kingdom of heaven is like a dragnet that was cast into the sea and gathered some of every kind [of fish], which, when it was full, they drew to shore" (Matt. 13:47–50). When applied to our parishes, this illustration provides a point of view that is both refreshing and challenging.

Consider the growth of the early Church. We learn from reading the Book of Acts that in time, "some of every kind" of people began to enter the Church. These newcomers were not Jewish. This led to a dispute about the need to keep Jewish law, which is recorded in Acts 15. Eventually the apostles had to ask themselves a question: "Does one have to be a Jew to be Christian?" In other words, the apostles wondered whether they needed to erect a barrier—or potentially tear down a bridge—and become a bit more selective.

In Galatians, we read how St. Paul struggled with this idea. In fact, it led to a confrontation with St. Peter: "But when I saw that they were not straightforward about the truth of the gospel, I said to Peter before *them* all, 'If you, being a Jew, live in the manner of Gentiles and not as the Jews, why do you compel Gentiles to live as Jews?'" (Gal. 2:14).

Eventually, the apostles, led by St. Peter, built a bridge: their response to this mounting tension was to declare that one need not first become a Jew in order to become a Christian (Acts 15:5–21). They courageously led the Church's growth by tearing down a barrier. Doing so meant that Jews and Gentiles would come to stand shoulder to shoulder in the Church.

Sometimes the barriers we erect are unintentional. We simply carry on with familiar ideas and actions without thinking about them. For example, one of the first things I noticed when I got to Saint Spyridon was a large sign that had been placed above the front doors.

The sign was blue and white—Greek people love these two colors, as you may know—and it read, "Greek Church of Northern Colorado."

The words struck me as problematic. Not far away was a Korean Presbyterian Church that I passed on my way to work. Whenever I drove by it, the thought that crossed my mind was, "That's the Korean church, and it is for Koreans." As I gazed at our sign, the same thought occurred to me—only this time, it applied to our parish. As people drove by, I am sure they were thinking, "That church is for Greek people, and I can't go because I'm not Greek."

I took down the sign. In retrospect, as we will discuss later, I should have moved a bit more carefully around making such changes. Removing the sign caused quite a stir among some of the people who had committed to forming this new parish. For some who were of Greek heritage, my action was hurtful. I remember a tearful conversation with one parishioner who felt something precious and essential was being taken away.

I can also recall a conversation with a prominent businessman in our community who had immigrated from Greece to Northern Colorado decades earlier. He too asked why I had removed the sign, along with the small Greek flags and figurines of Greek dancers that adorned our small fellowship space at the time.

"Well," I said to him, operating by a gut feeling, "I am not sure anyone up here knows what a Greek church is, and I suspect they simply think that a Greek church is for Greeks."

When our barriers are up, whatever they might be, it makes sense that church members expect others to look, act, and think like them to gain entrance into the church. When we build barriers as a community, then instead of growing in strength through welcoming and incorporating those we encounter (bridge building), we believe and promote potentially false ideas about what it means to be part of our Christian community.

Conversely, when we build a bridge, we remove ourselves from thinking that a specific identity or set of ideas will cause growth. In this state we embrace both the gospel and others who are not like us. Through bridges we can focus on an identity that is Christ-centered.

Developing a Sense of Urgency

In March of 2021 I was asked to speak at a clergy gathering for the Greek Orthodox Metropolis of Chicago. The theme was "Reclaiming the Great Commission: Strategies for Orthodox Evangelism in a Post-Pandemic World." In preparing for this talk I had requested several documents. One of them was the Greek Orthodox Metropolis of Chicago's "2020 Impact Report." On page 8 I read the following statement by the metropolis's registrar, Rev. Deacon Antonios Calash:

> The data and trends observed provide us with a picture of our Church, one in which fewer people partake in the "sacraments of initiation" today than in the past. If we continue on this downward trajectory, it is inevitable that we will have far more empty pews in our parishes. This not only means that our parishes may find themselves unable to support their basic operations and ministries, but more tragically, that there will be fewer Orthodox Christians witnessing to the Gospel and sharing the love of Christ in the world. One can surely point out that this downward trend is observed in most major faith communities across the United States. We cannot, however, afford to become complacent in this fact; we must understand the urgency of our reality. Instead of searching for excuses and becoming defensive, we should remain inquisitive.

The accompanying graphs told the same story in pictorial form. Deacon Antonios's statement stopped me in my tracks. In the years I have been speaking with church leaders, I had rarely encountered such an honest assessment of where we stand today.

Sadly, the drastic decline in membership is not restricted to Greek Orthodox parishes. From 2010 to 2020, the decline in Orthodox parish membership has crossed every geographical and jurisdictional line. Some declines are alarming. The Romanian Orthodox Church saw a decline of 44 percent in total adherents, while the Orthodox Church in America lost 13 percent of its membership.[8]

When looking at the registry statistics for the Greek Orthodox Archdiocese of America (GOA), we see the same alarming trends. The number of people entering the church has continued to decrease rapidly, and the same is true when we look at those getting married in our churches.[9] The only measurable increase in the GOA has been in the number of funerals.

Another self-study of Orthodoxy in America encompassing multiple jurisdictions has put the decline in the number of members within the church from 2010 to 2020 at a staggering 17 percent. This study notes a number of other troubling trends that demand our quick attention.[10]

Although these statistics are American, we assume these declines are occurring in other, increasingly secular parts of the world, including Orthodox countries. A sense of urgency is needed to address the shrinking Orthodox presence everywhere. And this urgency is necessary within individual parishes. In my situation, a variety of

---

8   "US Religion Census 2020: Dramatic Changes in American Orthodox Churches," https://orthodoxreality.org/wp-content/uploads/2021/03/2020Census-GeneralReport1.pdf

9   Source, Greek Orthodox Archdiocese of America, Registry Statistics 2016 Annual Report, https://www.goarch.org/-/2016-parish-registry-statistics?inheritRedirect=true. Unfortunately, at the time of publication the GOA has not released updated registry statistics.

10 "U.S. Religion Census 2020: A Decade of Dramatic Changes in American Orthodox Churches (2021)," https://orthodoxreality.org/reports/.

circumstances highlighted the need for change. As I mentioned earlier, before I arrived at Saint Spyridon the clock was ticking for me personally, since my bishop had told me he was going to reassign me after two years. My sense of urgency only increased after I arrived and looked carefully at our finances. I realized the parish didn't have enough cash to keep me employed for long. Additionally, a number of things needed to happen besides raising money. We needed to attract people, we needed to form ministries, we needed to buy a computer—the list of needs was long. All this was going to take time and leadership. I was going to have to learn quickly, and on the go, how to skillfully cultivate and guide our parish in a way that helped us accomplish a variety of tasks.

This meant I was going to have to make some tough choices and take some risks. I was going to have to focus on our lifesaving mission and set aside or prune certain ideas and initiatives that would not help us in the long run. But I was in good company: St. Paul felt the same sense of urgency. He wrote to the Christians in Rome, "And *do* this, knowing the time, that now *it is* high time to awake out of sleep; for now our salvation *is* nearer than when we *first* believed. The night is far spent, the day is at hand" (Rom. 13:11–12).

There is much we need to do to reclaim the Great Commission. In this we are greatly aided if we work with a sense of urgency. For me, the need to develop a rhythm in the life of the parish was exacerbated by what was going on around me. The building we purchased was a historic building, and, sadly, it used to be a church. All around me were buildings that *used* to be churches, and I understood what could happen to us if we failed to get to work.

You may recall Newton's First Law of Motion, which declares that an object at rest will remain at rest unless an outside force acts on it. Urgency is that force. It is something we apply to the system to get things moving.

When taking an honest look at your own parish, you might not have to look far to identify issues that need to be addressed urgently: declining attendance; older members but few if any young families; dwindling finances and perhaps the inability to pay a full-time priest or staff; few people willing to volunteer and lead; guests who show up but never return, or the lack of any guests at all. These issues are symptoms of deeper problems that need to be resolved before positive change can occur. At this point, the need for a sense of urgency becomes clear.

Urgency is powerful because it leads to action. It is like the spiritual discipline of sorrow, as St. Paul wrote: "For observe this very thing, that you sorrowed in a godly manner: What diligence it produced in you, *what* clearing *of yourselves, what* indignation, *what* fear, *what* vehement desire, *what* zeal, *what* vindication! In all *things* you proved yourselves to be clear in this matter" (2 Cor. 7:11). If you use urgency rightly, it brings repentance—heartfelt change. Without this urgency, we end up with the wrong type of worldly sorrow, which leads to death. We stay stuck, and contrition does not enter the picture. Contrition, along with urgency and godly sorrow, is like sitting on a sharp needle: it will cause you to jump up and act.

Urgency also accompanies us when we are in touch with the facts, when we are clear eyed about what is going on around us and in our communities. If we face the facts as I have been pointing them out, then inevitably we feel a rise in urgency. If, however, we remain with our heads buried in the sand, urgency is nowhere to be seen.

Sometimes leaders have to raise the level of urgency. As Archimedes famously said, "Give me a lever long enough and a fulcrum on which to place it, and I shall move the world." We don't have to run around crying "Fire!" But leaders have to apply some force—not an inordinate or crazy amount. We work to instill in ourselves and others a rhythm and a pace that is productive and positive. And if we use force like a lever, applying just enough and in the right place, things will begin to move.

Developing a sense of urgency inspires us to stretch ourselves a bit, reaching further than we have before. In the end, urgency helps us to get things moving in our community, and it is a worthy essential on our journey toward reclaiming the Great Commission.

I HOPE YOU ARE READY to turn the page with me and consider some additional steps we can take toward reclaiming the Great Commission. As we go forward, I encourage you to take with you our five essentials: regaining our sight, remembering our lifesaving mission, pruning, building bridges and not barriers, and developing a sense of urgency.

Review

Main Ideas

1. Barriers and opportunities are usually in plain sight.

2. Many parishes have lost sight of their mission.

3. Parishes fail to prune the activities and programs that are draining the community.

4. Building bridges instead of barriers is key to parish health.

5. The downward trend of growth in our communities should create a sense of urgency for all of us.

Action Items

1. If you are reading this as a group, begin this discussion with five minutes of silence focused on Christ.

2. Discuss: Do the worship, ministries, events, and programs of your community support Jesus' mission, embodied in His statement, "For the Son of Man has come to seek and to save that which was lost" (Luke 19:10)?

3. Discuss: Does your community understand Jesus' mission, and if so, in what way?

4. Invite someone new to come to your church, or, if you are reading this as a group, invite several new people to visit your Sunday Liturgy. At the end of the Liturgy, sit with your guests inside the nave and invite them to reflect on their experiences.

5. Invite various groups in your parish to do the same and to discuss what they have been experiencing in your community.

For Contemplation

1. Are we creating bridges in our community, and if so, can we identify them?

2. How do we make decisions about which ministries and projects we pursue?

3. What does autopilot look like in our parish?

4. Does our community inside the parish know what our mission is?

5. Do our neighbors know our mission?

6. If our doors were to close tomorrow, what would our neighbors say about our community?

PART II

Concepts of Parish Health & Common Barriers

CHAPTER THREE

Parish Health

ROUGHLY A DECADE into my time at Saint Spyridon, the Lily Foundation asked our parish to participate in a study. For the study, the foundation chose thirty Christian communities from the United States and Canada, representing many different Christian denominations. Of the thirty chosen, the only Orthodox church was Saint Spyridon. The two-year study attempted to understand why some parishes were growing and thriving, especially in an environment where the average number of churches in America that close annually is in the thousands.[11]

The pastors I met were incredibly thoughtful and dynamic Christian leaders. Unquestionably, their role was a major reason for their communities' success. (I will talk more about leadership in chapter 6.) Those two years gave me something invaluable: namely, time to

---

11 Data on church closings is hard to come by, since many denominations do not keep good records. However, one study from 2019 by Lifeway Research estimated that approximately 4,500 Protestant churches closed that year. https://lifewayresearch.com/2021/05/25/protestant-church-closures-outpace-openings-in-u-s/

process my experiences up to that point through listening and talking to others who were also leading a community.

One of the surprising things I learned was that our experiences were in many ways similar, even though our theology was very different. You see, most of the participants spoke in one way or another about the same reasons for their community's vibrancy and growth. In time, I came to place all these aspects of growth under the title "parish health." In the pages that follow, I will outline and define what this term means in greater detail.

I remember sitting, late one evening, with the pastor of one of the largest Presbyterian churches in the United States. I was telling her some of the things I was trying to do—ideas I thought were revolutionary—and I will never forget her response.

"Oh, it sounds like you're just being healthy."

During that time period, one email from a parishioner said something similar: "Dear Fr. Evan, Thank you for encouraging us to be normal and healthy." This did not strike me as high praise at first until I thought more about it. Healthy behaviors go a long way in changing our communities for the better.

In time, what I came to realize and then articulate is that what we were doing to grow and thrive in our parish of Saint Spyridon was simply an effort to be healthy. When I coupled this realization with the lesson I had learned from Fr. Elias about knowing what is and is not open to change, things started to come together for me. I think the concept of parish health is more profound than it first seems, as I hope to show in the pages that follow.

Remembering Who We Are

Much of what we do to reclaim the Great Commission is a process of remembering who we truly are. This truth is also at the root of the Christian story. Christ, the Church teaches, came to restore us to our right selves. In the story of our Fall found in Genesis, we learn that humanity lost something precious—our identity—when we fell away from God. We lost our true selves. The rest of the story in Holy Scripture is about how God attempts to bring us back to Him.

We learn this most poignantly in the Parable of the Prodigal Son (Luke 15:11–32). In the story we read about a son, the younger of two, who asks for and receives his inheritance early. This he takes from his loving father and squanders. In time the young man's condition grows desperate, and having nothing to live on, he finds work feeding pigs (v. 15). While working on the pig farm he sinks even further, wishing he could eat the slop he is giving to the swine (v. 16).

The story takes a dramatic turn in verse 17, when we read that the younger son "came to himself." Interestingly, we sense that the young man should have known all along what was right and who he was, but he had lost himself and thus his way. This is similar to the meaning of the goal of parish health in our churches. Our journey is about finding our true selves again. It is about recovering God's original plan and design for us.

Parish Health as Conceptual and Practical

In the previous chapter we learned about the five essentials on our journey of reclaiming the Great Commission. They are:

1. Regaining our sight
2. Remembering our lifesaving mission
3. Pruning
4. Building bridges, not barriers
5. Developing a sense of urgency

It is helpful to think of these essentials and other ideas presented in this book, such as the four concepts of parish health in the pages that follow, as tools that are both conceptual and practical. Parish health is not simply about writing down a practical list of steps and robotically pursuing them. For example, I cannot tell you how many times I have been on a call with a church leader discussing parish health only to hear him say, "Father, please just give us a list of your best practices. That's all we want!"

Nor can we say that parish health is simply conceptual, as if healthy parishes come about by remaining faithful to a set of ideas without taking concrete steps. I have also been on calls with parish leaders who have never gone beyond discussing the ideas of parish health.

Instead, we begin pursuing parish health as a means of reclaiming the Great Commission, attempting to graft the conceptual and practical into every fiber of our community's life. As we implement what we have learned, we do our best also to explain and discuss what we are doing within our community. This does not mean we need to do everything I or others recommend. Attempting to do so is a recipe for disaster, because we can easily become overwhelmed and lose our focus.

Moving forward in this way means we take a generous and positive approach to parish health. Something as small as moving a candle stand or as complex as beginning a leadership training program may help us to move the needle in a positive direction. In the Parable of the Talents, the Lord says to the faithful steward, "Well *done*, good and faithful servant; you were faithful over a few things, I will make you ruler over many things. Enter into the joy of your lord" (Matt. 25:21). We need to remember that God blesses even our small efforts. We trust the process, knowing that even a little movement is monumental and helps us build the needed momentum to take additional steps.

Parish Health Is Organic

We should also note as we get started that parish health needs to be organic to our community. The fundamental concepts will apply everywhere, but the specific application must grow naturally and uniquely within each parish. Parish health cannot be contrived. It must be *inside* us and the leaders we cultivate. For example, taking down a sign worked at Saint Spyridon, but it might not work for another parish. However, building bridges to ensure that everyone is welcomed is essential in all places.

In my parish we have found that focusing on outreach to the food-insecure is incredibly important, and we do have to stay vigilant in pruning away other activities to make this priority actionable. In another place, homelessness or education may be a priority. Pruning is needed there as well to make such an important focus possible.

Why Defining Parish Health Is Important

I have a cousin who is no longer part of the Church. One day we were discussing the Saint Spyridon community, and she was puzzled. What I was describing as "church" did not sound familiar to her. She had grown up in a parish that had a very different definition of itself from the one I was describing. It was as if we were talking about two entirely different things.

My cousin explained to me that she had never experienced any call to follow Christ or to put His teachings into practice. In fact, even after a childhood in a church, her understanding of the gospel was quite shaky. Shockingly, she had never participated in any outreach to those in need, and my cousin felt that the parish she grew up in had no real concern for the needs of the surrounding community. She had not experienced a sense of community and had not built any lasting relationships within that church. As you might expect, she no longer had a place in her life for Christianity and didn't see why anyone would.

This story may sound familiar to you. Perhaps you also have a friend or family member who is no longer part of the Church. Of course, we must be careful when analyzing my cousin's negative experience or anyone else's. A person may leave the Church for a variety of reasons, but hopefully it will not be because we have failed to be clear about who we are. And that's the funny thing—as she told me her story, I could not escape the feeling that this was exactly why she had left: her church had failed to be what we are called to be, and that was why she no longer "needed" Christianity.

This one example helps us understand why offering a definition for parish health is important. We may, however, be curious about how a failure to define ourselves occurs. Why was my community's definition so different from the one my cousin experienced? To explain how this happens, let's first look at a rather unusual teaching found in the Gospel of Matthew (12:43–45):

> When an unclean spirit goes out of a man, he goes through dry places, seeking rest, and finds none. Then he says, "I will return to my house from which I came." And when he comes, he finds *it* empty, swept, and put in order. Then he goes and takes with him seven other spirits more wicked than himself, and they enter and dwell there; and the last *state* of that man is worse than the first. So shall it also be with this wicked generation.

There are many ways to explain the meaning of this passage. However, one explanation helps us to understand what happens when we do not define parish health clearly for ourselves and our communities.

Each community is, in a sense, possessed. Now, unfortunately, we have come to view possession in a solely negative way, but perhaps we shouldn't. You see, the Church believes that, spiritually speaking, all people are possessed. The question is, by what or whom? The answer determines whether their possession is a good thing or not. For example, some people are possessed by greed or regret, others by gratitude and generosity. I think most of us would not choose greed and regret as the things that captivate our thoughts and hearts, but we'd gladly be consumed by gratitude and generosity.

The story from the Gospel illustrates this point by noting that when the man who had been possessed by an unclean spirit ends up dispossessed, this is, at first, a good thing. However, what happens next is important. The text says that after the demon left the man, it returned to find its former habitation "empty, swept, and put in order."

The man is now empty, or dispossessed, and thus he is ripe for the taking. The Church teaches us that if he has not been possessed again by something good, he remains unfilled—a void. This is a dangerous spiritual condition. Because the man remains empty, he is possessed again, but this time by "seven other spirits more wicked . . . and the last state of that man is worse than the first."

The same holds true for our parishes. In the absence of a positive definition of who we are, something else will take its place. Thus, when we fail to define clearly for our members who we are and how we operate—our identity—it is not only likely but definite that they or someone else will fill in the blanks.

This filling in will happen either incidentally or intentionally, and what fills this space may not be beneficial. Whether intentionally or not, a community can end up being defined by its politics, social agenda, or ethnicity. We can define ourselves as conservative or liberal, by our wealth or poverty, by our demographics, and so on. Each of these definitions is self-limiting and narrow. None of them is Christ- and gospel-centric.

We must be deliberate in defining who we are and what we are about if we wish to avoid the wrong definition taking over. If that happens, what begins to define health, and thus our identity, in our parish may be opposed to the Great Commission, and our community's latter state, as in the story, will become worse than its former.

One parish I visited defined itself as the "defender of Orthodoxy in the West." For them, the purpose of their community was to separate themselves clearly from what they perceived to be unorthodox belief and practice. On the surface, one might argue their goal was a worthy one. However, a closer look at what this definition really meant might lead to a different conclusion.

Jesus said, "And I, if I am lifted up from the earth, will draw all *peoples* to Myself" (John 12:32). Instead of drawing all people to Christ, this community's purpose had the opposite effect. The parish saw not only a reduction in its membership over time as long-standing parishioners left, but the surrounding people in their neighborhood showed no interest in joining, either. In fact, if I asked them whether people from the surrounding town had ever inquired into the Faith, the members would likely respond that such a possibility was unlikely, given the neighborhood's tendency to loose and impious living.

In the minds of any self-proclaimed defenders of Orthodoxy, few of their neighbors would be up to becoming Orthodox. Orthodoxy in this view is not something that can be shared. Their attitude was similar to that of the Pharisees and Sadducees of Jesus' day, whom Christ admonished in Matthew 23. These leaders placed spiritual burdens on the people that were too heavy or impossible to bear. Likewise, in this parish members believed that in their own practice of the Faith, they were "doing it right," and they viewed others as inferior or lukewarm Christians.

Lost in all of this, of course, is Christ's command in the Great Commission to bring the gospel to everyone, as well as His words,

"I have not come to call *the* righteous, but sinners, to repentance" (Luke 5:32).

When we lose sight of who we are and of Christ's call to us in the Great Commission, concepts and ideas creep in that disfigure us and make us unhealthy. This is one reason it is important to propose a definition of parish health and to study its four components. We need to be clear about this within our leadership and with our community as well.

As I noted above, I think my cousin left because of the way her community had come to define itself. Parish leaders had been possessed by ideas that were not positive, and while I don't think this happened intentionally, it led to her desire to have nothing to do with Christianity.

The Four Concepts of Parish Health

ONE: A Commitment to Christ and the Gospel (Orthodoxia)

In time, as the definition of parish health came to be more clearly formulated in my mind, I realized that placing Christ and the gospel first has to be primary. Unfortunately, when I thought about whether this had always been true at Saint Spyridon, I realized it had not. Even though I had left Denver to share Jesus and the gospel, I didn't always remain focused on doing so.

Writing this on paper seems odd. How can a Christian community not be about Christ and the gospel? In this failure, though, I am not alone. I remember speaking at a National Altar Boy Retreat that took place in Boston, Massachusetts. I was invited to give the keynote to several hundred young men and their parents on the opening night. I began my remarks by asking the question, "Who here has committed themselves to Christ?" Shockingly, only one person in that crowd raised their hand!

How often do we, like that crowd of altar boys, find ourselves forgetting our first love? It is true that we struggle to keep the first commandment to love God with all our heart, soul, and mind (Matt. 22:37–38). Having forgotten this commandment, we then fail in the second great commandment to love our neighbor as ourselves (Matt. 22:39). In the Book of Revelation, God chastises the church in Ephesus for forgetting their first love (Rev. 2:4–5). One could argue that the beginning of all sin is found in forgetting God.

When I struggle to stay focused, life in the parish becomes fragmented. This struggle is exacerbated by the distractions and the demands of the day. In such a state I found myself working on various tasks without a clear or cohesive plan. I was working hard, but progress became slow and diffused.

In time, I understood the need to get out of the daily grind on occasion. We must step out of our situations and learn the art of thinking strategically. This is something Christ did with His disciples. He would step away from their hectic ministry and review how things were going in order to redirect His followers (Luke 9:10). In this way, Christ stayed focused by staying in touch with what matters most.

In the end, our personal failure to hold true to a commitment to Christ and the gospel means our parish's purpose is poorly defined. This has led to the experience some of us have had of a Christian community that has lost its way and whose actions continually contradict this first component of health. A dear friend of mine, Fr. Theodore, likes to say that in such a state there is a gap between our statement of faith in Jesus and the way we live.

Orthodoxia literally means "right glory." It can also mean "correct belief" and "true worship." As Christians we should understand that in order to be truly transformed and changed for the better, we must be connected to right glory, correct belief, and true worship. This is why the first component of personal and parish health is a commitment to Christ and the gospel—orthodoxia.

The signs that point to our failure to hold true to this foundational commitment can be seen everywhere in our parishes. I would be remiss if I did not point out that in my travels around the United States, I have been struck by the fact that the largest events and projects in our communities are often not focused on Christ.

Time and again we pour precious resources—time, talent, and treasure—into events and causes that have little or nothing to do with the gospel: sports programs, food festivals, cultural preservation, language schools, dance programs, social gatherings, even political causes. Recognizing that our efforts are not focused on Christ and the gospel doesn't mean we must completely abandon our current projects. However, our newfound understanding should encourage us to think about how we might refocus and retool our communities to be totally Christ-centered. Getting there often means we take baby steps over time that lead to a shift in our priorities and our definition of who we are.

Over time, the first component of parish health—a commitment to Christ and the gospel—has to become our first objective. We want people to meet Jesus. This means that our first efforts toward healthy change must be constantly directed toward encouraging the people we encounter to develop a relationship with Him and to understand the Good News.

This is not easy, because we get distracted. We find ourselves arguing about music, language, carpet colors, and even seating arrangements for social gatherings. I remember debating which type of cookies could be sold at a bake sale. On one visit to a parish to help the community in reclaiming the Great Commission, I was told that most of the associate priest's time was taken up with arranging the youth basketball program. They came to realize that a priest should not be an athletic director but someone whose primary role is to point people to Christ. The basketball program was not a bad thing, but the resources it demanded were out of balance with the community's primary calling.

The truth is that these challenges will lessen when we focus on the first component of parish health, but the distractions will never go away. We need to remain vigilant. Thankfully, Jesus' words encourage us to stay focused: "Seek first the kingdom of God and His righteousness" (Matt. 6:33).

When we pursue parish health by committing first to Christ and the gospel, we can attempt to be a community that meets the deep spiritual needs of those already in our parish and of those we meet. This first component means that our goal is not growth. Our goal is not some small-t or big-T tradition, or even ethnic promotion and preservation. Our goal is Jesus Christ.

Experience has taught me that our foundational focus on Jesus Christ is not something we can ever leave to chance. Ironically, I have had people join our parish because they felt we were conservative, and others joined because we were liberal. I've seen people join because they like our music, the beauty of our sanctuary, or even my preaching! While these are all worthy things, they aren't the first reason any of us should be committed to a Christian community.

Thankfully, the liturgical tradition of the Orthodox Faith makes this same point. Each year we journey through the life of Christ in our celebration of specific feasts. These events are accompanied by prayers, hymns, and liturgical actions that are designed to do one thing: call the community back to a commitment to Jesus Christ and the gospel—to help us *remember our first love*.

You could ask yourself why we repeat this cycle every year. The obvious answer is that we need the reminders. Just as the coming of

Great Lent annually calls us back to a spiritual manner of living based in Christ and the gospel, so too does our liturgical cycle. It provides a continuous focus on this first concept of parish health.

In the early days of Saint Spyridon, and even more so today, when people talk to me about becoming members of our parish, I often say to them something like this: "As long as you are coming here to meet Christ, then we are on the right track. This place is about Jesus, and if by coming here you are growing closer to Him, well and good. But if not, don't stay. Keep moving until you find a place where you can."

Saint Paul had in mind this primary focus when he wrote about his time in Corinth in this way: "And I, brethren, when I came to you, did not come with excellence of speech or of wisdom declaring to you the testimony of God. For I determined not to know anything among you except Jesus Christ and Him crucified" (1 Cor. 2:1–2).

The Liturgy reminds us of this first love by stating emphatically, and more than once, "Let us commit ourselves and one another and our whole life unto Christ our God." To do this, we must follow our Lord's first public command: to repent. We must constantly renew our hearts and our minds in Jesus, and this prayer cannot be *stylized*—it must be *actualized* in our everyday lives.

TWO: A Commitment to Connecting Christ and the Gospel to Our Daily Lives (Orthopraxia)

When I was a young boy and did something on Sunday that was not in accordance with Christ, my grandmother would admonish me by saying, "My child, the taste of Communion is still on your lips. Think about what you are doing."

When I arrived at Saint Spyridon, we started three things on day one: We began to worship together on a regular basis. I started a Bible study on Tuesdays. And we began a Philoptochos ministry to demonstrate our "love of the poor." These three foundational activities—worshipping as a community, filling our minds with the Word of God, and serving others—were foundational steps in *orthopraxia*, living out our faith.

Orthopraxia means "right action"—right living, if you will. The word is related to *orthodoxia*, and it follows that right action grows out of right glory. In a healthy parish, each of us increasingly understands that simply listening to the truths of the gospel is not enough: "If someone says, 'I love God,' and hates his brother, he is a liar; for he who does not love his brother whom he has seen, how can he love God whom he has not seen?" (1 John 4:20).

In another place we read:

> For a good tree does not bear bad fruit, nor does a bad tree bear good fruit. For every tree is known by its own fruit. For *men* do not gather figs from thorns, nor do they gather grapes from a bramble bush. A good man out of the good treasure of his heart brings forth good; and an evil man out of the evil treasure of his heart brings forth evil. For out of the abundance of the heart his mouth speaks. But why do you call Me "Lord, Lord," and not do the things which I say? Whoever comes to Me, and hears My sayings and does them, I will show you whom he is like: He is like a man building a house, who dug deep and laid the foundation on the rock. And when the flood arose, the stream beat vehemently against that house, and could not shake it, for it was founded on the rock. But he who heard and did nothing is like a man who built a house on the earth without a foundation, against which the stream beat vehemently; and immediately it fell. And the ruin of that house was great. (Luke 6:43–49)

This second component of parish health encourages us to measure how healthy we are by the metric of how much of the gospel and our faith in Jesus Christ is lived out in our daily lives. Being a follower of Jesus means that what we do in our homes and the way we act as spouses, parents, siblings, students, employees, employers, members of the community at large—in the grocery line, as we travel or visit with people, and in the life of our community—must reflect that commitment.

> You are the salt of the earth; but if the salt loses its flavor, how shall it be seasoned? It is then good for nothing but to be thrown out and trampled underfoot by men.
>
> You are the light of the world. A city that is set on a hill cannot be hidden. Nor do they light a lamp and put it under a basket, but on a lampstand, and it gives light to all *who are* in the house. Let your light so shine before men, that they may see your good works and glorify your Father in heaven. (Matt. 5:13–16)

As a parish leader I try to ask parishioners and myself the following questions on a regular basis: "Does what Jesus said, taught, and did influence our lives? Is our parish different today than it was yesterday because we have applied to a greater extent our faith in Jesus and the gospel?"

> But when the Pharisees heard that He had silenced the Sadducees, they gathered together. Then one of them, a lawyer, asked *Him a question*, testing Him, and saying, "Teacher, which *is* the great commandment in the law?"
>
> Jesus said to him, "'You shall love the Lord your God with all your heart, with all your soul, and with all your mind.' This is *the* first and great commandment. And *the* second *is* like it: 'You

shall love your neighbor as yourself.' On these two command-
ments hang all the Law and the Prophets."

Jesus Christ's life was an incredibly disruptive force. If we have considered carefully and honestly what He taught, we are motivated to
change. With this knowledge in hand, a healthy parish constantly
challenges itself to consider more deeply the life of Jesus and how
members can incorporate His life into their own. In such a state we
not only work toward cultivating the fruit of the gospel in our parishioners' lives, we expect a harvest. When we define parish health in
this way and make the personal application clear, we no longer merely
hope to see the fruit of Christ in the hearts and actions of the people.
Instead, we witness its existence.

In the end, we must have the courage to discern whether or not
our people are applying the gospel to their lives. If not, then we must
pursue changing the health of our community by changing the way
we live.

THREE: A Commitment to Relationship Building and Forming a Spiritual Family (Koinonia)

One of the first questions I was asked when I arrived at Saint Spyridon was, "How long are you going to stay?" I told the handful of people who came to our first parish assembly, "I intend to leave my bones
here." I pointed to my oldest child, who was five at the time, and told
them that they were all going to be invited to her wedding.

I explained to them that I planned to baptize their children and
one day celebrate those children's weddings and see their families
grow up in the parish we built. Then I said, "We need to become a
family." At the time I didn't know that I was defining what it meant to
be a healthy parish, but in retrospect that is exactly what I was doing.

This idea leads us to our third component of parish health, which is found in the depth and quality of our relationships. In Acts 2:42 we read that Christians "continued steadfastly in the apostles' doctrine and fellowship." The original Greek word for "fellowship" is *koinonia*, which is used to indicate the deep and intimate relationships shared by a group of people. To a large degree, the quality and depth of our fellowship with one another impacts the strength and vibrancy of our community. We should also note that "doctrine" and "fellowship" are used in the same verse. This connection is played out in many parishes in the coffee hour that follows the Divine Liturgy. In this way, we keep a rhythm that the first followers of Jesus established, combining worship and fellowship into an almost seamless act.

Koinonia is realized when we foster a community setting in which people feel not only welcome but able to invest in one another's lives. Our Faith teaches us about a community of three Persons, the Holy Trinity. The Father, the Son, and the Holy Spirit live in a mutual and eternal movement of love for one another. This is not only our belief and a simple definition of trinitarian theology, but also a beautiful model for what it means to be a Christian community.

A healthy parish *is* a spiritual family:

Then Peter said, "See, we have left all and followed You." So He said to them, "Assuredly, I say to you, there is no one who has left house or parents or brothers or wife or children, for the sake of the kingdom of God, who shall not receive many times more in this present time, and in the age to come eternal life." (Luke 18:28–30)

Unquestionably, many of the members of Saint Spyridon have experienced a great deal of personal loss by choosing to follow Christ. Like St. Peter, they "left all." But a healthy community not only compensates for this loss, it builds a safe and loving home for those who find their way into its embrace. It becomes a community where people establish deep connections with one another. A spiritual family is a fabric of interwoven threads—individuals—that forms a unified whole—a family.

We could say it this way: a healthy church develops the bonds, the fellowship, the community, and the interconnected social interactions that imitate the Trinity. As I recalled my experience with the leaders of various Christian communities in the Lily Study, I realized that not one of these exceptional pastors ignored this truth. Rather, they all emphasized community and fostered it continually.

At the same time, a healthy parish makes room for others. A few years into my time at Saint Spyridon, one of our new members told me a story about visiting a parish during Holy Week. At the time he was a graduate student in a large metropolitan area away from his home. Being new to the area, he visited a cathedral parish for the services of that week. Because he was in attendance from the beginning of the week, when the number of people attending services was smaller, he became familiar with some older parishioners who sat in a specific row near the front. Being a student with an erratic schedule meant that he arrived late to Holy Friday services, when attendance in many places exceeds the capacity of the sanctuary. Standing at the back, he realized that he was going to remain there for the evening.

Not long into the service he noticed the familiar group of older ladies motioning him forward. Excited, he walked up and sat with them. Leaning over, he expressed in hushed tones his gratitude that they had saved him a seat. The lady closest to him leaned back and conspiratorially explained, "Yes, someone else sat down who we didn't know, but we kicked them out!"

Being healthy not only means we are a family, but it also means we make room for new family members. My own grandmother used to set a large table for holidays that often ended up being expanded midmeal to accommodate someone who hadn't had a place to go. Our parishes must operate similarly.

I realize the challenges that can come from this type of hospitality. Newcomers may not yet know or follow the "rules of the house," and they can cause members of the household to feel uncomfortable at first. This is normal. In time, guests operating in a healthy parish become part of the family, learning the rhythms and customs of their new home from their new brothers and sisters.

It is also true that every new member changes the makeup of the family. I have four children, and the arrival of each one changed the dynamics of our family. Those changes were positive, but they were also hard and required my wife and me to adjust to a new reality. It is important that we remember these lessons as we add new members. We must believe that there are no strangers in our spiritual family— only brothers and sisters we haven't met.

FOUR: A Commitment to Operational Excellence (Politeia)

During my first council meeting at Saint Spyridon, the treasurer gave a partial report of our finances. At the end of a series of questions he looked at me and said, "Father, I honestly don't know what the balance of our bank account is." I am not joking when I tell you that in my first few months, we often failed to deposit people's donations. Can you believe that? People would give us money, and we would fail to put it in the bank—not because we didn't need the money, but because our operational structure was poorly organized.

Parish health includes a commitment to operational excellence— *politeia*. In the classic sense, *politeia* is an ancient Greek word for the order of both social and political relationships in a town. Here it stands for the way we organize ourselves and govern and administer our community. It is our attempt to excel in leadership, organization, administration, and the structures that serve as a framework for everything that goes on in the church.

I came to realize that if we got the first three components of parish health right but failed in this last one, the people we served might give up on the parish. Look at it this way: If everyone is Christ focused and gospel focused, working at connecting their faith to their daily life, and prioritizing relationship and community building, but we forget to pay the bills or clean the bathrooms, people may stop coming, and things may fall apart.

Over the years, I have often ended up cleaning bathrooms or breaking out a can of paint to touch up a scuffed wall. Of course, pitching in and taking initiative is important, but more often than not my janitorial and handyman skills were tested because we had not organized roles and responsibilities in a way that would eliminate the need for me to add more tasks to my priestly duties.

Lacking operational excellence can also mean that we struggle to celebrate the divine services well. Our sermons may be poorly written and delivered, and we may sing off-key and without rehearsing. We need to work to develop technical competency in many areas, such as conducting efficient meetings and creating policies and procedures to guide our governance. These efforts go a long way toward building vibrant and growing parishes.

This reality reminds me of something Jesus said: "Woe to you, scribes and Pharisees, hypocrites! For you pay tithe of mint and anise and cummin, and have neglected the weightier *matters* of the law: justice and mercy and faith. These you ought to have done, without leaving the others undone" (Matt. 23:23). Likewise, healthy communities can't focus on the first three concepts of parish health alone. We need operational excellence too.

One way to talk about this last component is to understand the need for technical competency. If people are going to entrust to us the more important aspects of their lives, they first have to trust us with the most basic: "He who *is* faithful in *what is* least is faithful also in much; and he who is unjust in what is least is unjust also in much. Therefore if you have not been faithful in the unrighteous mammon, who will commit to your trust the true *riches*?" (Luke 16:10–11).

Consider Maslow's hierarchy of needs. If you have seen his pyramid, you know that at the bottom we find the basic physiological needs, such as water, food, and shelter, and at the top we find transcendence, or self-actualization—the place where we discover our full potential and even greater purpose. If we can't take care of the first level, we may find it impossible to get to the last. The same holds true in our communities.

I must say that when I talk about this fourth area, parish leaders often roll their eyes. Some protest, even stating that the church is not a business. Yes, they are right—of course the parish is not a business. However, common sense tells us we can't ignore operational excellence. We find the same concern in Holy Scripture. Saint Paul expected the bishops of the Church to be good managers of their own homes first before seeing to the oversight of a Christian community (1 Tim. 3:4).

Today the community of Saint Spyridon is still learning to lead courageously and communicate effectively. While I will say more about leadership in chapter 6, let me say a few words here. The art of leading well is learned over time. It would be dangerous for us to imagine that we have completed our training. Instead, our community has a longstanding commitment to learn, with each passing year, how to lead more effectively. We have attempted to host leadership classes on a regular basis while encouraging leadership discussions in ministry meetings, and we constantly attempt to learn about and apply new teachings while eliminating poor leadership behaviors.

This does not mean we are perfect or that we don't make mistakes. What is important, though, is the commitment to learning to lead well that is becoming a part of our parish's culture.

Our community is also continually learning how to communicate effectively. This means we attempt to utilize new online tools to hone our communication skills. We have attempted to create a more open, transparent, and two-way platform in the parish in which people can communicate with one another. We have also worked hard to operate with greater integrity and transparency. To this end, we have established policy and procedure manuals to help guide and define our decision-making and operating procedures. We undergo annual audits and share our financials regularly with community members.

Saint Spyridon is also working constantly on clarifying our vision and mission, roles, and responsibilities by periodically reviewing our strategic plan (a topic discussed in chapter 7). We print our goals in church publications and discuss them in ministry and team meetings. We build and refine organizational charts and define people's roles and responsibilities. We also have demonstrated fiscal responsibility and greater administrative order by setting up our budgets to meet our goals and ensuring that fiscal decisions are tied to actual financial capabilities and funds. At the same time, we make sure that our budgetary process and our reports align with our strategic plan—specifically, its vision and mission statements.

All of these commitments are aspects of operational excellence: to operate with integrity and transparency; to have clarity about our vision and mission, roles, and responsibilities; to show fiscal discipline and strive for greater administrative order. These are all works in progress and no doubt will be forever, but we are working diligently on them.

Summary

There you have it, the four concepts of parish health. Not one of them individually is enough. Just as the three spiritual disciplines of prayer, fasting, and almsgiving mentioned by the Lord in Matthew 5—7 work together in our spiritual growth, these four core values together define parish health. If we remove one, we risk the other three, and we lessen our opportunity to become a truly vibrant and sound parish.

» **Orthodoxia**—a personal & communal commitment to Christ and the gospel

» **Orthopraxia**—a personal & communal commitment to the transformation of our lives in Christ

» **Koinonia**—a personal & communal commitment to becoming a spiritual family

» **Politeia**—a personal & communal commitment to operational excellence

Working Toward a Shared Understanding of Parish Health

Have you ever witnessed an orchestra getting itself in tune? I remember going to the symphony with my mother for the first time as a child. We arrived early and entered the auditorium. Soon the musicians took their places and took up their instruments. I was confused at first as each of them seemed to be playing on their own. I heard scales played on different instruments, and no one seemed to be listening to anyone else. Then an oboe played a single note—I learned later it was A. Slowly, almost reverently, the rest of the instruments in the orchestra picked up that note. Now each musician was carefully tuning his or her instrument to match the oboe's pitch.

This may sound odd, but I found it beautiful, and I still do. There is something wonderful in hearing a symphony emerge from the initial cacophony of sound. And this is what defining parish health and working toward it over time can be like.

Saint Spyridon stumbled and bumbled in the beginning because I was not, and could not be, clear about what constituted parish health. My own uncertainty and the uncertainty of others meant that competing ideas crept in, and a type of cacophony prevailed. These ideas were not necessarily dangerous or harmful, but they consumed precious resources and stole our focus away from what should have been our priorities. I and the other leaders in the parish had to learn to define where we needed to go and why—and to keep our heads while doing so. At times our efforts felt like changing the tires on a moving car.

In the beginning, as parish leaders try to focus our attention and the attention of others on the concepts of parish health, things are hard. Just as with a rocket lifting off its pad, the larger part of the energy is needed during launch to get a community into orbit. Yet the task is far from impossible. One key component in our eventual success is the participation of parish leadership, who need to willingly engage and support the development of parish health concepts.

First and foremost, that means the parish priest. Like most community leaders, a parish priest has more to do than is possible. We often wear so many hats. We are expected to be teachers, preachers, worship leaders, father confessors, counselors, strategists, managers, fundraisers . . . and the list goes on. While juggling all these demands, a priest can easily lose sight of the core concepts of parish health. However, a mentor of mine continues to remind me that one of the key jobs of a leader is to think about his role and his goals, and respond accordingly.

Unfortunately, when we fail to think through our priorities, we can become reactive. Over time, being reactive can become a habit—plunging into whatever task presents itself with a focus that can be detrimental. My mentor is fond of describing this as ditchdigging, at which I excel. If you give me a shovel, I'll dig a trench that is deep, wide, and long. I'll also dig as many ditches as I can, often without thinking first of where I am going. "Get out of the ditch," my mentor would tell me, "and think about what you are doing."

Unlike digging ditches, leadership requires vision. It is about setting a tone and having a sense of where we need to go, not just managing where we are. We'll talk more about this later, but for now we need to recognize that a key component in getting a parish moving toward greater health is the commitment of its priest to do so.

The same goes for others who lead with us. Council members, ministry leaders, and committee chairs have to see parish health as a top responsibility as well. They can't become so focused on their tasks that they forget the mission. Several times a year now I sit down with the leaders of my community. One member of our leadership team who oversees fellowship told me that she often forgets the purpose of the work because of the sheer number of tasks that confront her (ditchdigging). In her defense, she oversees more than a hundred people, orders supplies, and creates lists and schedules.

But in a recent conversation we took a step back, which helped this leader realize that fellowship is central to becoming a spiritual family. It is not just about serving food and creating schedules. Without this clear definition of why the fellowship ministry is doing what it does, a leader can easily slip into becoming another ditchdigger. This may be okay for a time, but eventually, if we continue operating in this way, we may lose the heart and soul of our purpose.

Let me reemphasize an important point: Nothing in our communities will improve without a corresponding change first occurring in our leaders and in their behavior. Of course, people will resist what we do—they may even sabotage it. That's a given. But the first place of resistance is often in ourselves.

When I came to realize what the concepts of parish health were pushing me to do, I often reacted negatively at first by resisting the need for change. This still happens. In time we have to realize that this attitude gets us nowhere, and overcoming this resistance takes courage. My own inner reluctance reminds me of a World War II story from the book *Band of Brothers*.[12] Author Stephen E. Ambrose recounts the exceptional leadership of Captain Dick Winters of Easy Company. One particular story rings out in my mind when I consider the courage it takes to move forward with the concepts of parish health.

On June 12, 1945—a few days after D-Day, when the Allies landed on the coast of France to overthrow the Nazi regime—Easy Company approached the edge of a French village called Carentan. As they made their way down a road, they came under machine-gun fire and eventually mortar and tank fire. Quickly, almost instinctively, the company jumped into the ditches on the side of the road, looking for cover and digging into the earth with their fingernails. Soon their leader, Winters, was out of the ditch and on the road, calling for his company to get moving. He knew that if they stayed pinned down by their fear, they would die. To lead his men, he courageously got out of the ditch, put himself at risk by coming under fire, and began moving forward.

And in order to lead our communities, it is time for all of us to get going and move courageously forward to reclaim the Great Commission.

---

12   Stephen E. Ambrose, *Band of Brothers: E Company, 506th Regiment, 101st Airborne from Normandy to Hiltler's Nest* (New York: Simon and Schuster, 2001), 89–107.

Review

Main Ideas

1. Each community must approach parish health as a combination of the practical and conceptual.

2. Lasting change comes about organically. It must come from inside us and the leaders we cultivate.

3. If we fail to define our communities, something else will. Ideas and projects will disfigure the parish and make it unhealthy.

4. We must always remember our first love and constantly direct the people we encounter to a commitment to Christ and the gospel.

5. A healthy community is invested in one another's lives. It is a spiritual family and always makes room for newcomers along with those within.

6. Operational excellence finds its roots in the Holy Scriptures and is necessary for a parish to reach its full potential.

7. When the parish works together to improve its health, it sets the tone for where it needs to go, rather than just managing where it is now.

Action Items

1. Interview active and inactive parishioners. Ask them, "When you think of a healthy parish, what does it look like?" Collate and discuss responses to see if you notice any trends.

2. Review the four components of parish health and discuss how you might begin to implement them in your community's life.

3. Ask people on the team to gather and investigate resources that can assist your church in developing greater parish health. (Note: Resources exist within and outside our communities.)

Discuss them and decide which ones to use. Remember, God is at work in your community.

For Contemplation

1. Examine how the four components of parish health are present in your personal walk with Jesus and write a short reflection on each:

   » Christ and the gospel

   » Christ and the gospel in my daily life

   » Relationship building and forming a spiritual family

   » Operational excellence

2. Spend time as a group confidentially sharing your reflections.

CHAPTER FOUR

Common Barriers, Part I

Leadership Issues and Unbalanced Identity

L EADING A COMMUNITY is not easy. So many important things require our attention. The Great Commission should be our priority, but for many of us it is not. When it isn't, we have to ask ourselves why this is so and attempt to understand how we have failed.

With these questions in mind, we can assess the distance between these two poles: where we are and where we should be. The gap that exists between our fulfilling of the Great Commission and our current state is made up, to a large degree, of the barriers we face or may even have erected ourselves. These are the barriers that keep us from reclaiming the Great Commission.

Becoming a healthy parish over time is made possible in large measure by a process of barrier breaking that works alongside the positive changes we implement. It is vital that parish leaders within our communities take on this responsibility of dismantling barriers so that the communities they lead can experience a new level of vibrancy and growth.

Discussions about Barriers

Before we begin the actual work of dismantling barriers, we need to go through a process of discovery and analysis. Often in this initial stage, we—both leaders and those being led—can become defensive. But as community leaders we have a responsibility to guide this process to a positive outcome. We can achieve this by doing a bit of work on the front end.

I know from personal experience and many years of pastoral counseling that when conflict is handled wrongly, we often begin voicing our concerns by attacking, accusing, or criticizing others. When this happens, the person or group we attack becomes defensive. In response to their self-defense, we up the ante and dig in our heels by stereotyping their decisions and behaviors unfairly, even to the level of showing contempt for their ideas. This escalation of the conflict leads to a breakdown in dialogue. At this point, we shut down and shut ourselves off from one another, thus ending the opportunity for meaningful communication. Sadly, this means we will not come to understand and learn from one another.

I call this negative conflict cycle the "rocket launch" sequence of negative conflict. Once you have pressed the attack–accuse–criticize button, you have launched yourself into the response of defend–stereotype–show contempt, which leads to each side shutting off from the other. The reason we enter into this negative form of conflict is simple: we believe that our point of view is right and the other's is wrong. Tragically, even if this is true, such a pattern of negative conflict does not lead to building consensus, shared support, and mutual understanding.

Therefore, it is helpful for leaders to set the ground rules for how we will ask questions and discuss our barriers. Prior to our conversations about sometimes difficult topics, we should model the way we will speak to one another. These types of "conversation covenants" are constructive in getting us to talk in a way that leads us forward. At the bare minimum I suggest communities commit to being *open* with one another, *respectful* of one another, *curious* about other people's perspectives and experiences, and personally *accountable* for their words, their position, and their place in the story. An easy way to remember these four points is through the acronym ORCA: open, respectful, curious, and accountable.

I believe communities should commit to handling their conflicts using this ORCA model. It can be written down as a pledge and signed. We do this with our parish council at Saint Spyridon. Additionally, we continually share the concepts when we meet or when we are going to discuss a difficult topic. Many of my parishioners have posted this positive conflict model on their refrigerators.

Deep down, both leaders and those we lead understand the value of looking at our barriers to parish health. Intuitively, we know that certain issues must be dealt with, and the unhealthy parts of our community's life can't be ignored if we hope to reclaim the Great Commission. But we can't allow our discussions to fall into a list of our grievances and complaints. That will not help. It is better to question, discuss, and describe effectively and honestly what holds us back. Then as leaders we can develop, as we will discuss later, a plan to address what ails us.

Understanding the Five Barriers to Parish Health

It is important for you to understand at the outset that it would be difficult and of little use for me to try to detail every type of barrier parishes face. Just as a map that listed every ditch and gully would be unusable for actual navigation, so is an exhaustive list of barriers. Rather, what helps is to become familiar with the general concept of barriers and some of the more common types. Then your leadership team can examine your community, together and with the help of the members of your parish. You will likely find examples in your own parish of some of the issues described here. You will also find other barriers that may be specific to your community. Either way, the next step is to design a plan to dismantle them. In chapter 7, I provide an outline of a parish health plan that your parish can use. Keep in mind that your knowledge and understanding of your community, its circumstances, history, and context play an essential role at every stage.

Don't forget the cardinal rule that change in our communities begins with ourselves as leaders. This idea is essential to the concept of parish health and to our own spiritual health. In reality, the two depend on each other. Our Lord teaches this principle: "Why do you look at the speck in your brother's eye, but do not consider the plank in your own eye?" (Matt. 7:3). Jesus reminds us to begin with ourselves and to avoid the temptation to place the blame on someone else.

Barrier #1: Undeveloped Leadership

To a degree, every parish shows strong health in certain areas, but no parish is perfect. This means that every community has areas that are and will remain undeveloped. The important distinction we need to make is that when the key part of the parish's structure, *its leaders*, remains undeveloped over the long term, this lack of leadership builds an almost insurmountable barrier to that parish's health. It becomes like a skeleton without a spine.

The reasons our communities suffer under poor leadership are many. Most likely, though, the cause lies in our failure to develop effective leaders. The truth is that leaders are, for the most part, not born but made.

This is not what I initially believed. When my bishop sent me to Saint Spyridon, I would have argued that I was in fact a leader, and in the most basic sense of the word, that was true. Yet in retrospect, I was not a very good or developed leader. When I look back over my earliest decisions, I frequently cringe, as I am sure I will in five years when I look at those I am making now. Leadership is something we learn over time and with help.

For example, as an undeveloped leader, I wrongly assumed it was my responsibility to show up for every meeting and oversee every decision. I would attend meeting after meeting, and my weeks were filled with appointments that left me exhausted. As I learned the art of leadership through a great deal of study and coaching, I came to understand that this style of leadership was undeveloped.

There were several problems with leading in this way. For one, it left the cadre of leaders in my parish undeveloped, undeployed, and subservient to me. Further, it meant that they felt micromanaged and powerless to make meaningful decisions. Over time they no longer felt enthusiastic or empowered to guide and lead the ministries they had been entrusted with. Additionally, it meant I had to be everywhere at once and always ready with a solution.

I remember feeling a great deal of anxiety about letting go. To me, stepping back and letting others lead seemed too risky. I wanted to make sure I had control of what happened, thus ensuring nothing would go wrong. Thankfully, through study and mentoring I came to understand the value of vision and strategy setting. This allowed me to step away from direct oversight and control of the various aspects of the community's life. Instead, as I learned to set and share the strategy and the vision with the leaders in the community, I could step down—and they could step up. This happened because the entire group of leaders shared the vision, and they were able to add not only their support but their creativity and energy to developing the vision in the parish in ways that went beyond my limited abilities.

It is fascinating to consider Christ's ministry in light of this idea. When we examine the time period the Gospels recount, we realize that for three years Jesus actively trained the leadership of the Church. This was His main task.

Healthy parishes imitate Christ in this respect, encouraging and assisting their leaders to grow and develop. They invest in training their leaders and see the important connection between good leadership and overall community health. In our parish, we have brought in outside experts in the area of leadership to hold retreats on the subject. We set aside time during meetings to discuss ways to lead more effectively. I meet regularly with the various leaders in the community, and we discuss and develop their leadership skills. I have purchased books for them, sent them podcasts, and shared my own experiences.

On a personal level, healthy leaders understand the importance of developing their skills. They realize that leadership is learned and that this learning goes on continuously. A level of self-awareness and self-examination helps them to see their own limitations, and it compels them to grow and to seek help.

These types of leaders cultivate the ability to see their blind spots or find trustworthy people to help them do so. They compensate and augment their abilities, not by covering up their weaknesses but by growing and finding others who can assist in areas where they are less capable.

Seven years into my time at Saint Spyridon, I asked someone in my community to sit down and discuss with me my abilities as a leader. I wasn't looking for someone to simply tell me what he or she thought I wanted to hear. Rather, I was looking for an honest, educated, and critical review. What I received was more than I had hoped for, even though much of it was hard to hear. Thankfully, the person I asked was willing to help, and I was patient with myself but willing to address the items that had been brought up.

This was just another step in my development as a leader. Part of what came up in these discussions was my inability to see my own shortcomings. This is to be expected. Most of us are myopic when it comes to self-assessment. I was encouraged to develop a more reflective and detached view of my leadership. This approach was familiar to me, given my own participation in the process of repentance and confession in the Church. Many times I had taken a critical view of my spiritual life, and I had learned to confess my sins. Similarly, I was being asked to take a careful look at myself as a leader and to assess my skills and my shortcomings with the help of others.

I was also advised to recruit and encourage others in the community to lead alongside me—especially people who had skill sets I did not. Over time, I have recruited people for various tasks, such as caring for and overseeing the sanctuary space, running our spiritual formation program, and developing leadership training. I've also hired a highly trained bookkeeper. In the end, this process of self-assessment and recruitment has made the community much more vibrant.

Barrier #2: Leaders without a Plan

The second main barrier found in our communities arises when we lack a clear plan. Having a plan and being clear about our purpose is an effective leader's second responsibility (after his or her own personal development).

However, when I share the idea of a clear plan in one of my presentations, I often receive a fair amount of pushback. Many Christians believe that faith and planning are mutually exclusive. This perspective is, in my view, naïve.

I understand God's working in human history as logical—planned, if you will. Galatians 4:4–5 tells us that He ordains times and seasons: "But when the fullness of the time had come, God sent forth His Son, born of a woman, born under the law, to redeem those who were under the law, that we might receive the adoption as sons." God makes plans to bless us ("For I know the plans I have for you, declares the LORD, plans for welfare and not for evil, to give you a future and a hope" [Jer. 29:11 ESV]), and Romans 8:28 assures us that "all things work together for good to those who love God, to those who are the called according to *His* purpose."

Jesus Christ is called the Logos, a word which implies divine reason, order, and meaning. Saint Luke notes that a chief reason for writing his Gospel was to give an orderly account (Luke 1:3). Later in this same Gospel we learn that a dishonest man is commended for his dishonest but shrewd and calculated dealings with his master. The Lord then laments the lack of planning found among His followers: "So the master commended the unjust steward because he had dealt shrewdly. For the sons of this world are more shrewd in their generation than the sons of light" (Luke 16:8). In the end, I think we should set aside any feelings of discomfort when it comes to discussing and implementing planning in our parishes.

There is no doubt that God has entrusted to us a sacred and holy task, the building up and ordering of His Church. This responsibility becomes clear in the Sacrament of Ordination to the priesthood. After the bishop lays his hands on the candidate for priesthood and he is ordained, the bread and wine are consecrated, then the new priest is given the holy Body of Christ to hold in his hands. The bishop takes the Body, places it in a communion cloth, and directs the newly ordained priest to stand at the back of the altar. The bishop instructs him to safeguard and faithfully keep the Eucharist and protect it until the Lord requires it of him on the Day of Judgment. Later, this same bread, now become the Body of Christ, is placed in the chalice and distributed to the faithful gathered at the Liturgy.

Similarly, those of us who comprise the laity in the Church make up the royal priesthood, and like the ordained clergy, we have a sacred obligation to care for the Body of Christ that is the Church. We are stewards who have been entrusted by God with the right ordering of our mission in the world. Careful and thoughtful planning is the right response to such an eternal and important duty, and we all bear a measure of responsibility to see that it is done.

Strategic planning helps us ask and answer some fundamental questions—primarily, "Why are we here?" "Where do we want to go?" and "How are we going to get there?" In this process we examine our strengths, weaknesses, and opportunities. In developing a plan, we are forced to ask these tough questions that often have not been asked—questions that need to be answered if we are going to get on the road to reclaiming the Great Commission.

Communities without a strategic plan have no vision or mission. These parishes have poorly defined organizational and administrative structures. In such a state, they lack clarity about people's roles and responsibilities, which causes confusion and redundancy.

Without clear direction, we often drift from our main purpose, and irrelevant and detrimental ideas can become our priority. Vision and mission setting help us clarify our purpose and our plan, bringing focus to the community. When elements of the Great Commission are included in our vision and mission, we recalibrate the development and creation of our ministries as well as worship and community building. Additionally, when we develop organizational structure with clarity about who fills which roles and responsibilities, people work more efficiently and with less conflict.

I saw this firsthand when Saint Spyridon considered building a new facility to accommodate our growing parish. At first, our vision, mission, and organizational structure were lacking. As a result, our property search was haphazard and unfocused. We investigated and vetted many properties that were unacceptable, wasting lots of time and money, which increased the level of frustration among those conducting the search. Additionally, because we had not properly organized ourselves and defined roles and responsibilities, people stepped on one another's toes, made decisions for the community without being commissioned to do so, and operated independently instead of cohesively.

This rather chaotic way of operating was unnecessary. When one ministry leader knows what another ministry leader oversees, there is greater collaboration and symbiosis. At the same time, organizational structure helps all of us understand how we meet our vision and mission and where our weak spots are.

In short, the community that lacks organizational or technical competency doesn't know why it is doing what it is doing or how to do it. These communities rarely excel in the fourth concept of parish health, operational excellence. In the end, it is the leadership's job to ensure that our communities have a plan, which greatly reduces these kinds of problems.

In my view, strategic planning is positive and proactive. Ultimately, strategic planning is a tool that provides some of the detail we need to understand and remove the barriers that stand in our way. I will discuss strategic planning and where this process fits into our overall plan in more detail in chapter 7, "Creating a Parish Health Plan."

A Few Symptoms of Undeveloped Leadership & Lack of Planning

- » The community fails to see the importance of training its leaders.
- » Leaders fail to develop themselves in the area of leadership and other areas as well, including their own spirituality.

» The community does not see the connection between parish health and good leadership.

» Leaders do not understand their purpose and role.

» Leaders do not spend time planning and goal setting.

» Leaders remain technically incompetent, getting things wrong.

» The community has trouble making decisions and following through.

» The community does not retain good leaders.

» The community fails to set up structures that are transcendent—that will outlive the current leadership regime and be capable of furthering the parish's identity and mission.

» Members refuse to follow the leadership due to a lack of trust in them and their abilities.

» Confusion persists about people's roles and responsibilities.

» The talent within the community leaves the playing field or sits on the bench: they quit serving out of frustration and discouragement, or their gifts are not utilized.

» Lacking focus, the parish expends limited resources on nonessential tasks.

» The community is continually putting out fires, addressing immediate needs but not moving forward.

» Decisions are not implemented; nothing really changes because of lack of follow-through and discipline.

» Year after year, things just stay the same.

Barrier #3: Unbalanced Identity

A parish whose leaders fail to place Christ and the gospel first is unbalanced. This failure results in the loss of the parish's identity, because the community becomes fixated on the nonessential. Over time, these parishes will develop reasons to protect and promote what is unimportant. They will even elevate the nonessential and label it sacred.

This language is not hyperbolic. Think of Israel's devotion to the golden calf in Exodus 32, or King Nebuchadnezzar's maniacal devotion to his statue in Daniel 3.

I have visited a number of parishes that are unbalanced. One particular large urban parish comes to mind. After experiencing steady decline in membership, ministry support and creation, and financial support for over a decade, this parish decided it needed to take action. The leadership's response was, however, unbalanced.

A bit of an explanation of their situation is helpful. Not only had the parish experienced these declines, but the neighborhood around it had also changed. Economically the area had become depressed, and what had been a thriving upper-middle to middle-class neighborhood had deteriorated. In time, cars in the parking lot were being vandalized during Sunday services. In the minds of the leaders, this economic decline had led to the parish's decline, when in actuality it was due to other factors. To counteract the fall-off in vibrancy and growth, the parish decided to invest in fencing and security. They did not give any thought to engaging the community and neighborhood around them or to developing ministries to meet the economic challenges their neighbors were facing.

Another midsized parish I worked with had undergone similar declines. In order to change the trajectory of the parish, they decided to turn a home next door that the parish owned into a museum that honored their history and heritage. In the view of the leadership, this would attract new people who would be interested in the community's long presence in the area and its ethnic culture. They did not even consider the idea that an emphasis on evangelism and the sharing of the gospel would bring new members.

This loss of focus on the Great Commission is also evident on a broader, systemic level. I have visited with leaders of dioceses and metropolises who have attempted to retain the large number of youth who leave the Church by organizing sporting and cultural events. In fact, in many parts of the country these sporting and cultural events are the largest efforts of the dioceses and metropolises in terms of financial commitments and numbers of people involved. There is a persistent belief that these events will attract youth and families back to the Church, even though no data exists to support these beliefs.

Simply put, an unbalanced identity arises when the leaders of our communities fail to keep themselves and others focused on the Great Commission. Let's examine why and how this lack of focus occurs in our leaders and subsequently in those they lead.

External Opposition

One way opposition enters our lives is from the outside. In our attempt to stay faithful to Christ and the Great Commission, certain forces oppose us. Saint Peter warns us to "be sober, be vigilant; because your adversary the devil walks about like a roaring lion, seeking whom he may devour" (1 Pet. 5:8). Evil is real, and it is opposed to good. It seeks to destabilize and destroy. With this in mind, a Christian takes into account the malevolent power of Satan and realizes that the evil one will work to destabilize our parishes by confusing our leaders about their primary responsibility.

One community that had worked hard at removing its barriers told me that this effort had led to new growth. Most of that growth had come from a rather young demographic. As a result, the parish experienced a baby boom. Unfortunately, the older, established membership of this parish felt that the babies and children of these young families were loud and disruptive to the services on Sunday.

They also felt that the parents of these children did not have a proper respect for the sanctity of the services, nor did they adequately supervise their children.

While there is much to be said about incorporating new families and proper behavior in the divine services on a Sunday, the danger exists of losing sight of the good that is occurring in the midst of our community when barriers are removed. Instead, the evil one seeks to stir up division and discord and pit us against one another. In this instance, the board and leadership initially admonished parents, posted signs, made announcements, and encouraged the removal of children from worship.

The Church takes seriously the subject of spiritual warfare. In the beginning of the Sacrament of Baptism, we pray for those about to enter the Church. We read aloud a series of exorcism prayers. These prayers acknowledge the existence of evil and its influence in the world. We pray over those about to be baptized or chrismated, asking for God's protection and assistance in overcoming and defeating Satan. As these prayers conclude, we ask those seeking membership in the Church to publicly renounce Satan and spit on him. After this, we turn toward Christ and enter the sanctuary, publicly affirming our faith in Jesus and the gospel.

The same actions found in the beginning of the baptismal service are required of us as we seek to remove the barrier of unbalanced identity from our parishes. Our efforts begin in our own hearts. Leaders must acknowledge the constant necessity of recalibrating ourselves and our communities toward Christ, the gospel, and the Great Commission. Doing this leads to a balanced identity. These words may seem a bit harsh. However, if we look to our liturgical tradition, we note how often we are asked to do this very thing.

For example, several times in the Divine Liturgy we hear the prayer, "Let us commit ourselves and one another and our whole life to Christ our God." This reminder is read aloud each Sunday, and it stands as a call to return to Christ and to focus on Him. We are also invited at other times throughout the liturgical year to refocus ourselves on Christ. One of my favorite instances comes during Holy Week, when we are invited to come forward during a Holy Thursday service and venerate the Cross of Christ. In this liturgical action we are asked to consider the great sacrifice Christ has made for us through His death, and how important it is to us. Our Lord and the saints of the Church know how hard it is to keep our identity clear.

Internal Opposition

Unbalanced identity also arises from within. All believers—and especially leaders—who have made a commitment to walk in Christ at their baptism find it difficult to do so. We allow distractions in our lives to take precedence over God, leading to an imbalance in us and in our communities. Jesus, in the Parable of the Sower, describes these internal barriers in this way:

> Therefore, hear the parable of the Sower: When anyone hears the word of the kingdom, and does not understand *it*, then the wicked *one* comes and snatches away what was sown in his heart. This is he who received the seed by the wayside. But he who received the seed on stony places, this is he who hears the word and immediately receives it with joy; yet he has no root in himself but endures only for a while. For when tribulation or persecution arises because of the word, immediately he stumbles. Now he who received seed among the thorns is he who hears the word, and the cares of this world and the deceitfulness of riches choke the word, and he becomes unfruitful. (Matt. 13:18–22)

In other words, Jesus is saying that many things arise in our own hearts that lead us away from staying balanced and fruitful in Him. These internal struggles cause us to lose sight of our identity and our desire to keep the essential in its place of prominence.

In another place in Holy Scripture, St. Paul describes the internal challenges we face:

> As you therefore have received Christ Jesus the Lord, so walk in Him, rooted, and built up in Him and established in the faith, as you have been taught, abounding in it with thanksgiving. Beware lest anyone cheat you through philosophy and empty deceit, according to the tradition of men, according to the basic principles of the world, and not according to Christ. For in Him dwells all the fullness of the Godhead bodily; and you are complete in Him, who is the head of all principality and power. (Col. 2:6–10)

In the end, as St. Paul makes clear, no leader—and therefore, no community—is immune from losing sight of our identity, our purpose, and what is essential. However, healthy leaders remain focused on Christ and the Great Commission through whatever ups and downs may come their way.

False Identities

When leaders fail in this essential task, an unbalanced identity becomes their community's way of being. Such parishes learn to live in a type of compromise with the gospel that is unhealthy—a compromise that leads to caving in to special interests.

For example, a parish may operate with the understanding that new members need to look and act a certain way or become something they cannot be in order to enter the Church. This, as we learned earlier, is not a new problem. The apostles, the leaders of the early Church, for a time also lost sight of their true identity and purpose, as well as of the need to keep what is essential first. They failed to remain focused on the Great Commission. Instead, they started to require people to become Jews before they could become Christians. The leaders, and thus those who followed them in the early Church, began to promote and protect a special interest—namely, the requirement to keep specific Jewish traditions—over and above the essential and universal call to Christ and the gospel.

An example of this in today's world, as mentioned earlier, occurs when a sports program begins to dominate youth programming, or when cultural events dominate the life of the parish, even displacing worship. One particular case I studied in a large parish was rather scary. This community annually spent tens of thousands of dollars on a folk-dance program for its youth and poured hundreds of hours into training its dancers. Meanwhile, its church school was underfunded and poorly attended. On a visit to this parish, I noticed that during Sunday Liturgy the church was virtually empty until the very end, when parents and youth poured in. I was confused by this and asked why this was happening. I was told that the dancers were "required to attend" Liturgy to remain in the dance group.

In another parish, attendance in their language school had skyrocketed, which pleased the leaders. When I asked them about worship attendance, I received a different answer: very few of the youth in that community, or of those enrolled in the language school, were present in church or Sunday school. As I noted earlier, this same imbalance occurs at higher levels of the Church, at diocesan and archdiocesan levels, where certain activities are given attention and precedence over and above a relationship with Christ and living out the gospel and the Great Commission.

Confusing Nonessentials with the Essential

Once again, imbalance isn't a new problem. We find a similar situation in the Book of Acts:

> Now in those days, when *the number of* the disciples was multiplying, there arose a complaint against the Hebrews by the Hellenists, because their widows were neglected in the daily distribution. Then the twelve summoned the multitude of the disciples and said, "It is not desirable that we should leave the word of God and serve tables." (Acts 6:1–2)

In this situation, the apostles remained clear about what was essential: their role in spreading the gospel. But sometimes a misguided leader will set aside his or her essential role as it relates to the Word of God and wait tables (figuratively speaking) instead. Worse, leaders within this type of system can end up defending the indefensible and label any attempts to dismantle such nonessential programs as counter to the parish's identity and even the gospel! Remember here the example from Galatians 2, when St. Paul confronted St. Peter about separating himself from the Gentiles during meals. In my experience, when I questioned the budgetary priorities of the parish that invested heavily in folk dancing and not in religious formation and education, I quickly got the sense from the clergy and parish leaders that I was going where I was not invited.

The folk-dance program of this parish was, in their view, holy and could not be questioned. It was central to the community's life and identity. In the other community, when I wondered aloud why the youth and parents supported the language program with such fervor but were uninterested in worship or Sunday school, I was told that the language program was a "sacred obligation"—the actual phrase they used. In fact, the leaders hoped that involvement in the language school would lead people into faith in Christ. How odd it is to think that we'd start with preaching and teaching something other than the gospel in order to bring people to the gospel!

Some might argue that language schools, dance programs, and other projects enrich the life of our communities. However, they often displace what is essential. We must recognize that the way we deploy our limited resources matters. First things must come first. I am reminded of what St. Paul told the Christians in Corinth: "All things are lawful for me, but not all things are helpful; all things are lawful for me, but not all things edify" (1 Cor. 10:23). The same is true today. We have to consider carefully what we plant, for this is what we will harvest.

It may help us at this stage to recognize that many of these types of barriers have been inherited. They are "small-t" traditions, not Holy Tradition. And they are not always compatible with the Great Commission or our attempts to reclaim it.

> Brethren, if a man is overtaken in any trespass, you who *are* spiritual restore such a one in a spirit of gentleness, considering yourself lest you also be tempted. Bear one another's burdens, and so fulfill the law of Christ. For if anyone thinks himself to be something, when he is nothing, he deceives himself. But let each one examine his own work, and then he will have rejoicing in himself alone, and not in another. For each one shall bear his own load.
>
> Let him who is taught the word share in all good things with him who teaches.
>
> Do not be deceived, God is not mocked; for whatever a man sows, that he will also reap. For he who sows to his flesh will of the flesh reap corruption, but he who sows to the Spirit will of the Spirit reap everlasting life. And let us not grow weary

while doing good, for in due season we shall reap if we do not lose heart. Therefore, as we have opportunity, let us do good to all, especially to those who are of the household of faith. (Gal. 6:1–10)

These words of St. Paul encourage us. He reminds us of the leaders' responsibility to restore and correct their communities when they become unbalanced. He knows that what we do and our persistent focus on Christ, the gospel, and the Great Commission will have an impact in the future on the spiritual state of the Church and the harvesting of souls for God's Kingdom.

"Us" and "Them"

When we look closely, we find that unbalanced parishes live in silos: They group people into categories and predetermine who can become part of the community. One community leader told me that a church he served in the South unofficially expected its members to be white and Republican to attend. Parishes may even persist in such attitudes when new people and new ideas find their way inside. One parish leader told me that after his church had begun working on breaking down this specific barrier of exclusivity, their efforts had indeed led to growth and new vitality. But during a later visit, he expressed concern over this new phenomenon. "Father," he said to me, "I was hoping we'd grow, but not with *these* types of people. They are so different from us!"

Herb Brooks faced similar feelings when coaching the US men's hockey team that won the gold medal at the 1980 Winter Olympics in Lake Placid, New York. After assembling a number of players from different universities, he struggled at first to get them to see the essential: they now played for the same team, the United States. For a time, one overriding factor inhibited their play and their growth:

they saw themselves not as teammates of the US men's hockey team but as players of their respective universities. Initially they even defended their specific outlook as sacred: the players continued to fight and hold grudges against one another based on their respective schools. Once they embraced their identity as Team USA, they worked together and won the gold.

In parishes that have broken through this barrier of "us" and "them," we find health. They are vital and growing in many ways. These communities are diverse. They experience new people joining because they love Jesus, not because they married someone in the parish, happen to like the sports program, or enjoy the food.

Diversity leads to new ideas and new ways surfacing, and these new ideas and ways don't come only from the new people. Rather, balanced communities have unlocked the potential already present in their parishioners.

In 2020, in the midst of the COVID-19 outbreak, people in Saint Spyridon, in our town, and throughout the world were suffering on many levels. In my years of ministry, however, I have never been more in awe of the people who make up our parish. In a rather short period of time, they responded in ways that were both creative and powerful. In the hope of inspiring you, let me share a few ways they responded to the crisis that was unfolding around them.

A COVID-19 relief fund was established with over $50,000 to meet financial needs. The parish formed a small committee, generated a form, and posted it on our website. Parishioners were invited to apply on behalf of themselves or of people they knew who were suffering financial hardship. Checks were cut over the next two years for rent, groceries, tuition, medical payments, and other needs, and the funds for meeting these needs never ran low.

The pandemic also increased homelessness in our town, and another group in the parish began working with a local relief organization to house homeless families. Parishioners compiled funds and resources and participated for over a year and a half in housing families who were struggling to get back on their feet during this time.

One additional response was international. Some members of our community had retired and moved to Ecuador. There, during the pandemic, they noticed that food insecurity had increased exponentially. As a result, we started a food relief program for Ecuador that began delivering over ninety family meal kits per week.

These examples prove that diversity is positive. Without numerous ideas and perspectives, it is unlikely that any of these efforts would have taken place. In contrast, in a parish suffering from an unbalanced identity, the talent within their midst is usually disengaged, refusing to pool resources and ideas to participate in meaningful ways.

Of course, dismantling this identity barrier is far from easy. In Acts 10 we read about St. Peter's vision, which challenged him to preach the gospel to non-Jews. At first Peter recoils from the idea. He says he cannot share the gospel with those who are unclean. God quickly corrects him, telling St. Peter that he cannot call unclean what God has made clean. In other words, St. Peter is told that the gospel is for everyone, and as Ss. Cyril and Methodius, St. Nino of Georgia, St. Nicholas of Japan, and many other missionary saints have shown us, this is the essential mission of the Church.

Moving away from an unbalanced identity cannot happen overnight. It requires time, gentle pressure, and wise, caring leaders. Using the core concepts of parish health will help, as well as acknowledging and understanding this barrier and discussing it in our communities. Additional resources are needed, and the next chapters will provide them.

A Few Symptoms of an Unbalanced Identity

» Devotion to Christ and the gospel is not central to the life of the community.

» Christian identity is replaced by some other identity.

» Parishioners don't know or have forgotten who they truly are.

» Nonessential(s) replace the essential.

» Leaders support and defend the nonessential(s).

» The Church's true values are compromised, and leaders cave to special interests.

» The parish's false identity becomes an idol and is even considered sacred.

» Anyone who tries to dismantle the idol is opposed.

» Evangelism vanishes—the Great Commission is replaced by the Great Omission.

» Worship becomes anemic and secondary to other activities.

» Spiritual maturity does not materialize in members.

» Members emphasize their differences from others, and "us versus them" dominates any conversations about change.

» The first three core concepts of parish health are missing: commitments to Christ and the gospel, to connecting faith and daily life, and to relationships and community building.

» The parish becomes irrelevant to their neighbors and the world and fails to serve them in a meaningful way.

» The community is not diverse; instead, they preselect, prejudge, and presort who can join.

» The community is characterized by what they are not instead of what they believe.

» The parish becomes smaller and smaller over time, lacking vitality and growth.

» Newcomers remain visitors and do not stay; guests are not welcomed.

» New people and new ideas aren't given a chance.

Review

Main Ideas

1. Setting ground rules for honest dialogue is crucial for discovery and analysis. We should establish a conversation covenant based on the principles of ORCA (Open, Respectful, Curious, and Accountable).

2. Positive change in our community begins with a healthy, effective leadership team.

3. Christ's earthly ministry had a strong emphasis on developing leaders.

4. Strategic planning answers the key questions: Why are we here? Where do we want to go? How are we going to get there?

5. Nonessential activities can become sacred to us and replace our essential task of reclaiming the Great Commission.

Action Items

1. Implement a conversation covenant for your leadership team and community using ORCA principles.

2. Take time to carefully reflect on:

» Your parish's leadership style and competency, assessing and evaluating their strengths and weaknesses.

» Your community's vision and mission.

» Your community's barriers, paying special attention to where your parish has replaced the essential with nonessentials.

For Contemplation

1. What nonessentials have become sacred for your community, and in what ways have they replaced what is essential?

2. Write in your journal about the culture of your parish. What do you notice?

3. How can you begin a dialogue about the barriers you have identified?

CHAPTER FIVE

Common Barriers, Part II

Resistance, Sabotage, and Stagnation

Barrier #4: Resistance & Sabotage

BACK IN 2007 when I arrived at Saint Spyridon, I wish I had known about the inevitability of resistance and sabotage. Naively, I did not account for these incredibly corrosive and powerful barriers that stand in the way of reclaiming the Great Commission.

Resistance

Resistance occurs when people push back against implementing changes. They may be doubtful about the expected benefits, or they may actively disagree that a specific change is needed or even a worthwhile idea. The problem may stem from poor communication about the reasons behind the changes or from a lack of understanding about the Church's identity and purpose. Resistance can also come from emotional causes: fear of change, sentimentality about the status quo, or reluctance to put in the work required to implement a fresh vision.

Whatever the reasons, the reality is that no matter the place, the size, the age, or the relative health of our parishes, we should expect to find resistance at every stage. Even in a young community like Saint Spyridon, these responses accompany the journey. They are found at every level of the church, in everyone: in ourselves, the clergy, ministry leaders, council members, parishioners, bishops, councils, dioceses, metropolises, and the archdiocese.

Not too long ago, our leadership introduced a new idea in the area of giving. For years, our parish had been sending out annual pledge/stewardship cards to our members at the close of the year. On these forms, they told us how much they would be donating to the parish in the coming year. After some study of the issue, our giving team became convinced that this system was flawed in several ways. After some time discussing and developing ideas, they presented their new concepts to the leadership of the parish. The leaders resisted.

The giving team suggested doing away with the annual stewardship drive and the cards. But this simple change was outside the customs and norms our parish had followed for over a decade. The people in leadership were fearful that by doing away with the cards, we'd lose financial support and the ability to accurately create the budget for the next year. People raised these objections and several others, even though research showed us that this new system would lead to greater giving—a fact that proved to be true in the years after we implemented this change.

Strategic Reasons behind Resistance

Providing a clear vision and mission to our parishes is an essential first step in avoiding resistance and even sabotage. This is not to say that when such guidance and discussion occur, resistance evaporates or fails to materialize. However, sometimes resistance begins and then persists because we have failed to clearly communicate the reasons certain changes are being implemented. The process of articulating and gaining support for the parish's vision and mission is an important one. (Chapters 6 and 7 discuss in greater detail how we go about developing and sharing them.)

When we find ourselves facing resistance, there is likely a lack of understanding and support for our vision and mission as a parish or ministry. This has happened in my community a number of times. Most recently, in one of our small group ministries, the leader noticed a growing level of resistance to the policies and goals among the members. Her first thought was to clamp down and demand that members adhere to the established rhythms of this ministry—reacting with some tactical changes and short-term fixes.

I suggested something different. Using the soft approach described below, I encouraged this ministry leader to begin a process of resharing and reshaping the vision and mission by sitting down and discussing things with the ministry's constituency. In my mind, the problem of resistance in this case had arisen from a lack of understanding and agreement around the ministry's purpose and goals. So it only made sense for the leader and its members to gather and go through a series of discussions that reconnected everyone with the vision and mission and with one another. This took some time, but it helped us avoid having the resistance grow and become open rebellion.

Emotional Reasons behind Resistance

One of the reasons resistance arises is cultural. Here I don't mean something to do with being Serbian or Romanian. Rather, within our churches, certain norms and customs emerge over time, and it is natural that the culture of the parish becomes used to doing things a certain way. When we introduce a change, we are altering the community's habits. Resistance is a natural response.

Another reason people resist our efforts is fear of the unknown. Fear is a particularly powerful emotional response. When we make changes, we are moving from something we know to something we do not. This introduces a new level of uncertainty. We can no longer predict the results that will follow. In changing our giving program, Saint Spyridon entered uncharted waters—off the map, with its familiar landmarks. For us, the introduction of a new way of doing things was scary and caused a great deal of anxiety and fear. In this state our parishes become stuck, and we have allowed fear to control our decisions.

We also resist positive change because we worry about violating the Holy Traditions of the Church. It is important to remember here that changing the teachings of the Faith—those things that should remain unchangeable—is not what this book is about. As you may recall from the Introduction, Fr. Elias was elated that our area clergy were locked in a discussion about paperwork and not about the Divinity of Christ.

This fear of disregarding Holy Tradition arose at Saint Spyridon when we made positive changes to the music we used in the Divine Liturgy. Some within the community had wrongly assumed that the music we were using was Traditional with a capital "T"—and therefore unalterable. This was not true, as a great variety of music and small-t musical traditions exists in the Orthodox Church.

Additionally, we resist new ideas because of the wrongheaded notions and conclusions our communities have reached over time. These are often the nonessentials that we protect at all costs, as already discussed. We believe these things are our mission, but they are not.

Sabotage

Sabotage is the most aggressive form of resistance. While resistance comes in many forms, most of it is not dangerous to the health of the community. Sabotage, however, is always destructive and dangerous. Sabotage is willful obstruction—those seeking to sabotage you are looking to destroy what you are doing.

It may be helpful to mention that sabotage can grow out of resistance, or it can even be someone's starting place in response to change. It may also be beneficial to know that sabotage arises for the same reasons as resistance. The challenge, of course, is that sabotage is not open to a new direction or dialogue. It is not simply closed off; it is corrosive. It seeks not only to hinder but to defy and dismantle.

Sabotage is not simply a refusal to be under another's guidance, vision, and authority. It is rebellion and self-direction without regard for others or the community. We can think of Lucifer's fall. Or the actions of Judas. When confronted with the reality that Judas was not just resisting Jesus but attempting to sabotage Him, Jesus cut him loose: "And having dipped the bread, He gave *it* to Judas Iscariot, *the son* of Simon. Now after the piece of bread, Satan entered him. Then Jesus said to him, 'What you do, do quickly'" (John 13:26–27).

For a much more innocuous example of sabotage, let's consider my decision during the early days of Saint Spyridon to push the candle stand against the wall and place welcoming ushers to the side. Let's say an usher didn't like the idea. He had grown up in a traditional parish with the narthex set up a certain way, and he believed our parish had no right to mess with this small-t tradition. So each Sunday he pushes the candle stand away from the wall and stands behind it.

This is sabotage—taking action to disregard a directive and to foil the effort to change. Will the parish disintegrate because of a few feet of floor space in either direction? Of course not. But even this small example of defiance is indicative of a larger problem—a refusal to work with others and to submit to leaders' directives. This is active undermining. It is subversive—a cancerous attitude expressed in physical action.

Resistance and sabotage, like the other barriers, cannot be ignored. In the case of resistance, leaders must recognize what they face and then work diligently and patiently to remove it. But sabotage is different. I would not be patient with sabotage. Instead, it requires quick and decisive action. This action, of course, must remain connected to our Faith and our obedience to Christ. It must be taken in a way that imitates the example of Christ the Good Shepherd. However, He was not indecisive or patient with sabotage. Recall His exchange with Peter:

> From that time Jesus began to show to His disciples that He must go to Jerusalem, and suffer many things from the elders and chief priests and scribes, and be killed, and be raised the third day.
>
> Then Peter took Him aside and began to rebuke Him, saying, "Far be it from You, Lord; this shall not happen to You!"
>
> But He turned and said to Peter, "Get behind Me, Satan! You are an offense to Me, for you are not mindful of the things of God, but the things of men." (Matt. 16:21–23)

Your leadership team is not perfect. None of us is. We will make mistakes as we seek to align our community with the Great Commission. But as we remain faithful, prayerfully and thoughtfully taking steps to welcome people into the Church and to help everyone to grow closer to Christ, we as leaders need to keep focused on the goal of parish health. When community members resist the call to be the Church rather than a social club—and even actively seek to undermine our efforts—we must stand firm.

Dealing with Our Own Inner Resistance

Of course, overcoming resistance and sabotage is an essential task of leadership, if we hope to continue moving our community in the right direction. But it is wise to understand that removing these barriers does not occur overnight. It will take time, persistence, and, most of all, good leadership. So how do we go about it?

I believe that overcoming resistance and sabotage begins with the acknowledgment that it is part of the process of reclaiming the Great Commission. The next step is to recognize resistance in myself. This is an important step for leaders. I have to consider how I might be obstructing positive change. It is possible that I am not willing to put in the required work and self-examination to see clearly my own resistance. It could be that it is much easier to stay where I am and to remain in a state of comfortable resistance instead of moving to the uncomfortable position of looking at something new. It is difficult to stay on the journey that requires me to look carefully at my own values, mission, and vision, as well as the community's. This examination results in asking the question, "Why am I doing what I am doing?"

Symptoms of Resistance & Sabotage

- » People refuse, resist, or oppose following authority and/or the decisions the leadership of the parish has made.

- » They show up late for, undermine, or are absent from meetings.

- » They refuse to cooperate or even to verbally agree to cooperate.

- » They take on a role in parish leadership but do not deliver on their assigned tasks or meet agreed-upon deadlines.

- » They intentionally make mistakes or sabotage the efforts of others.

» They work behind leaders' backs and do not support the group's decisions.

» They exhibit passive-aggressive behavior.

  ◊ They indirectly express negative feelings but don't put them on the table openly to discuss them.

  ◊ They agree publicly but not privately.

  ◊ They signal agreement, but when the work begins, they abstain, fail to deliver, or become aggressive.

» They sow dissent or discord with others.

» They sit in meetings with a frown and exhibit poor body language or a poor attitude.

» They work without passion and are listless.

» They are critical, throwing grenades.

» They offer critiques but do not offer solutions.

» They work with emotions but not facts.

» They get stuck on minutiae and minor details, dying on hills and not mountains.

» Their minds are made up, period.

» They are interested in analysis paralysis.

» They are happy to discuss but not to act.

» They often work in assumptions, not reality.

» Their actions are fear based.

» When they speak, they may say, "A lot of people in the parish feel . . .," which is likely code talk for "I feel this way."

» They give the impression that they have a lot of support for their views, but they don't want to take the step yet of saying how they personally feel.

Dealing with Resistance in the Community

As we work to dismantle the barrier of resistance and sabotage, we make a game plan to address it. We acknowledge that breaking down these barriers takes time, careful observation, hard work, and lots of courage and grit.

Below I offer a simple, step-by-step plan to overcome resistance and sabotage in our communities.

1. Use and deploy the skill set of a developed leader (see chapter 6).

2. Carefully observe and note what is occurring in yourself and the community.

3. Take what you have learned from your observations and use your notes to identify and assess the problems you are facing.

4. Based on your identification and assessment, determine your response to resistance and sabotage: the soft approach or the hard approach (described below).

5. Move slowly, deliberately, and prayerfully. Remember that getting people to change is not about shoving your ideas down their throats.

The Soft Approach to Overcoming Resistance & Sabotage

The soft approach seeks to overcome resistance and sabotage in a methodical and positive way. It is based on the following assumptions:

» We believe this is the approach Christ used to overcome resistance in most instances of His ministry.

» We believe and hope people can and will change in time and adopt the new way of doing things in the parish.

» We are not ready to give up trying to bring them along.

» We believe this approach will result in broad-based support within the community for the changes we are implementing.

The soft approach assumes goodwill in the hearts of resistant people, and this is important. The saints warn us to be careful about judging others. We don't know their stories, and someone who is causing division in the parish might be carrying inner wounds that we can't see. Listening ears and open hearts can make a world of difference in winning over such a person. So, we start here.

Steps in the Soft Approach

Step 1: Invite people to tell you what they feel and think, listening carefully to what they tell you.

> » We begin by encouraging people to talk to us. We listen actively to them and avoid making assumptions about how they feel and why they are resisting change. Instead, we work diligently to make sure we understand where the resistance is coming from and why. We make sure we are hearing what people are saying to us, and we may deploy the response, "Let me tell you what I heard you say . . ." Ultimately, we are trying to understand what is in the hearts and minds of those resisting change. We attempt to answer the question, "What is their resistance telling me?"

> » We also listen carefully to the ways community members are speaking to one another. What do they say in their conversations about suggested changes? What do these conversations tell us about the resistance in the community?

Step 2: Have a healthy dialogue.

> » After listening, we should be in a position to have a healthy dialogue. We need to make sure there is an honest exchange of ideas, not a conversation where one person pretends to listen, but what is said goes in one ear and out the other.

> » This is the perfect place to deploy a conversation covenant and the ORCA method. (See p. 101.)

» The goal is, once again, to understand what is going on in the heart and mind of the other.

Step 3: Make your case. Provide compelling reasons for the changes you are implementing.

» In this step we attempt to win people over through providing the evidence for our new way of operating.

◊ This is not a sales job or the marketing of an idea; nor are we trying to force a false agreement.

◊ Rather, we are sincerely and openly sharing our heart and our vision with people. We are making our case for what we believe to be right and painting the picture for them of where we believe we need to go to reclaim the Great Commission.

◊ Another way of saying this is that we are telling the story and trying to convince others that the journey we are going on is worthwhile. In doing this we are attempting to enlarge the hearts and minds of those we lead.

» Provide whatever information you can about the ideas and the destination. Explain the goals and objectives you are trying to achieve by making the changes you have suggested.

» Give them the opportunity to respond, react, and learn from what you have presented.

» If someone remains on the fence or in opposition, ask them:

◊ "How do you propose we improve the program or go about making changes?"

◊ "What are your ideas?"

Step 4: After some progress with steps 1–3, try to bring people into the tent and make them ambassadors of your plan.

» Get the community, including those who had been resisting, on your team.

» Deploy people you believe can help you increase support in the community.

» Work to bring more and more of the community on board with the ideas being presented, and seek to make them enthusiastic supporters of what you are doing.

The Hard Approach to Overcoming Resistance and Sabotage

Unfortunately, after thoughtfully and prayerfully using the soft approach, leaders may find that some people will not budge. They may be vocal in their objections, they may be quiet and passive-aggressive in their disagreement with the direction of leadership, or a little bit of both. But if you are facing sabotage, you have to put a stop to it. You can't and shouldn't work with an individual or a group who is trying to undermine your efforts. You can attempt to deploy the soft approach, but most likely you will have to deploy the hard one. Each approach has risks and rewards.

The hard approach seeks to overcome resistance and sabotage in a straightforward and confrontational manner. To put it bluntly, the message this approach conveys is "my way or the highway," or "get in line or get out." It is based on the following assumptions:

» We believe that Christ utilized this approach when He faced persistent and entrenched opposition.

» We have attempted to overcome resistance and sabotage through using the soft approach and have failed.

» We have determined through careful observation that what we are facing is entrenched, persistent, irrational, and long-term resistance and sabotage.

» We have weighed the costs and have determined that in order to move forward, we must accept a certain amount of loss in support, and this cannot be avoided.

Steps in the Hard Approach

I have kept these steps simple and succinct. Due to the corrosive reality of sabotage, it must be dealt with simply, quickly, and decisively.

Step 1: Identify and determine that what you are facing is entrenched resistance and sabotage.

» Leadership should initiate this step only after the soft approach has not resulted in bringing the person or group on board with parish changes.

» In most cases when sabotage has been identified, you should notify those who are above you in the chain of command. For a priest, this would be the bishop or his representative. In the case of a ministry leader, it may be the parish board or priest.

Step 2: Isolate and meet with saboteurs individually or in a small group.

» We should never choose a public venue for a difficult conversation. We are followers of Christ, not cowboys engaging in a showdown at the O.K. Corral.

» The Prayer for the Beginning of the Day from the Optina Elders includes the petition, "Teach me to act firmly and wisely, without embittering and embarrassing others." A private conversation is preferable to possible public humiliation.

» I highly recommend having someone with you when you conduct this meeting. This is not only a biblical principle but a wise step. Choose someone whom you respect, trust, and love to accompany you. This person should also be someone who is respected, trusted, and loved within your community. It also helps if this person is viewed as fair and nonpartisan. Here we are not thinking of how the saboteurs will receive their presence as much as how those within the community will respond if they question who accompanied you when the meeting took place.

Step 3: Describe accurately and fairly what has occurred. Stick to the facts and refrain from emotional or accusatory statements.

Step 4: Clarify your expectations for those sabotaging your efforts.

» Let me be clear: in the hard approach we are not opening a new dialogue. You have already offered the saboteur(s) that opportunity in the soft approach. Instead, you are clarifying in black and white what your expectations are with regard to their future behavior. We must ensure that there is no ambiguity. It is best if our expectations are specific and simple.

Step 5: Ask them to cease and desist their efforts of sabotage immediately. We do not provide additional time for the saboteur's actions to stop.

Step 6: Ask for their unconditional support.

Step 7: If their support and agreement is not given, ask them to remove themselves from the community.

Barrier #5: Stagnation

The barrier of stagnation is a disfigured, inward focus and refusal to change. When we begin stagnating as a community, we build barriers by thinking first of serving ourselves. As a result, we can become parochial, narrow-minded, and closed off to the world around us. We can begin to idolize our past and view most change as dangerous or even heretical.

The image I have in my head for this barrier is a stagnant pool of water. Stagnating water, as you may know, does not have an inflow of fresh water, nor does it have an outflow. Instead, the water in the pool festers. Because it is not continually oxygenated, the health and quality of the water declines.

Stagnant Pools

This decline is occurring in the Great Salt Lake in Utah. Over time both the inflow and outflow of this lake have decreased. As it has shrunk, its salinity has increased, and the variety and abundance of life within it has almost vanished. Today only four things can live in the Great Salt Lake: algae, bacteria, brine shrimp, and brine flies.

Likewise, a stagnating community loses diversity and lacks the virtue of hospitality even to those from within their own tribe. Leaders lose sight of the Great Commission, and in its place they focus their attention on their community's own interests, causes, and needs. These unhealthy parishes go about designing worship, ministries, and programs for internal consumption only.

Such parishes can be focused on various types of social gatherings and self-promotion, such as events and dinners. One large parish holds several banquets throughout the year. These galas are held to entertain their own membership and to celebrate the parish itself. Of course, such events can be a normal and healthy part of a community's life, but they should not be its central activities. These events foster the sentiment of exclusivity, which may include the belief that the parish is somehow special, set apart, and truly unique.

In contrast to this, in the miracles Jesus performed, we notice that the beneficiaries of God's action are not only those who were healed, forgiven, restored, or comforted, but also the bystanders and the community at large. We see this in the miracle of the Samaritan woman Jesus met by the well in John 4, in the exorcism of the Gadarene demoniac in Mark 5, and in the restoration of Zacchaeus, who climbed the sycamore tree in Luke 19. In all three instances, the townspeople who knew the person came to meet Christ as well. They benefited from His presence and His restoration of someone among them. This is essential for us to remember as we design, build, and develop the life of our parishes.

In His ministry, Jesus likewise worked to bring light to those in darkness (Matt. 4:15–20; Luke 5:32) and to serve those who did not yet know Him (Luke 19:10; Acts 13:47). In communities that are healthy and living according to the example Jesus set for us, people outside the community are welcomed and invited to "come receive the Light."

Leaders in healthy communities think of others first, even when they are hosting a dinner or fundraiser. They avoid the barrier of stagnation by working hard to ensure that the members of the church remain engaged in the community and the world around them. This results in a healthier community that is interested in, focused on, and generous toward others.

For example, the Philoptochos ministry in a large Colorado parish sponsors an annual fundraiser called Tables Extraordinaire, a popular event among GOA churches. Volunteers decorate tables and chairs with beautiful, Christmas-themed place settings and decorations, and visitors buy tickets to view the tables and attend teas and a banquet. All proceeds go to local charities.

Tables Extraordinaire is the year's largest Philoptochos fundraiser for this parish, and traditionally the banquet included an ornament exchange among attendees. A few years ago, the leadership decided to abandon this small-t tradition and instead asked guests to offer monetary donations that would be split among four local ministries, including an outreach to homeless youth. The result exceeded all expectations: more than fifteen thousand additional dollars were donated for those in need. And any guest who really needed another Christmas ornament could stop by Target on the way home.

In contrast, a stagnating parish does not look outward. As in the lifesaving station parable from earlier in the book, these parishes will go to great lengths to keep from getting involved in the community around them. They will, figuratively speaking, build outbuildings and farm out care for the community's needs by enlisting other agencies and people to serve those needing help.

Of course, donating to local charities is a positive thing—a way to leverage the expertise around us rather than reinventing the wheel every time a need comes up. But writing checks should not be a parish's only form of outreach. It is possible to give money while also removing ourselves from the opportunity to connect with the needs of the people around us. If we refrain from engaging our communities, developing connections, or even showing interest in what the community cares about, we will begin to stagnate. One way to measure whether we are stagnating is to ask the following question: "If our community were to cease to exist, would anyone besides our own members notice?"

Fresh Water

A major problem in stagnating parishes is a lack of the fresh water that comes from new people and new ideas. This barrier means that communities are unable to move the needle toward greater health, growth, and vitality because they lack the demographic and idea diversity to do so.

In stagnating communities, a single dominant characteristic prevails among the members. This lack of diversity can be found in a type of religious puritanism or small-o orthodoxy of beliefs that is unhealthy, such as the singularity of a certain race, ethnicity, or socioeconomic status, or a set of devoutly held ideologies. The community may enforce passively—or even explicitly—a certain outlook or way of thinking, and as a result, visitors sense they need to be a particular type of person to be accepted.

This barrier of stagnation is related to the barrier of unbalanced identity, when parish members develop an "us versus them" mentality. An unbalanced identity leads to a parish limited to its dominant characteristic, resulting in stagnation. People who visit may realize that they don't look or think like the people in the parish, or that the parish doesn't look like the surrounding community, so they don't stay. Visiting or staying in a parish like this is intimidating. Newcomers may feel they are destined to remain outsiders who can never fit in or become what the other members of this church already are.

Across the United States, Orthodox parishes like this exist. They have failed to engage the neighborhood and the people who live next door. Over time, they find that their members have moved far from the parish's location, so they close their doors and move to a new neighborhood.

Stagnating parishes miss out on the blessings of the fresh input and perspectives that new people bring. Diversity is a strength. We can see its importance in the natural world through one of the hobbies I truly enjoy: fly-fishing. It is a nuanced and challenging sport. Over the years I have learned that fish like diverse waterways. River trout that inhabit the streams and rivers of the Rocky Mountains live in cold, flowing rivers with boulders, downed logs, underwater plants, and overhanging willows. These features and others result in biodiversity, with good places to spawn and hide from predators. It also means the fish are healthier, grow larger, and, most importantly, are challenging and fun to catch! Featureless rivers do not result in healthy and numerous populations of fish.

Not far from my house, a river was ruined by a massive flood that washed out bridges, altered the flow of the water, scoured the river bottom of its logs and boulders, destroyed the habitat of birds and insects, and released pollutants that damaged the entire ecosystem. The restoration of the river will take many years and will require the regrowth of various aquatic and land plants, as well as underwater features that were wiped out, before the fish will return.

Similarly, developing the fresh water of diversity in our

communities is hard work that requires attention and time. In recalling my parish's response to the COVID-19 crisis, I see a direct connection to this point. The attention we gave to building up diversity over time led to creativity in a time of crisis. A more stagnant community is unable to meet new challenges with such flexibility and innovation. Again, when I use the word "diversity," I am not calling for Orthodox Christians to consider a way of life that abandons unchanging truths or fails to invite people to repent. Instead, I am highlighting the fact that Christianity has always celebrated its wide variety of saints and rejoiced in their diverse backgrounds and circumstances.

Our Commonality with Others: We Are All Sinners!

Diversity means that the people entering our parishes will have problems, including struggles with sin. Christianity has also given the sinner a place to be transformed. In our communities, we should exhibit a level of gentleness and humility toward others that is therapeutic. Consider the Parable of the Wheat and the Tares in the Gospel of Matthew. The truth is, the one thing you have in common with the person next to you is that you are both sinners!

Another parable He put forth to them, saying: "The kingdom of heaven is like a man who sowed good seed in his field; but while men slept, his enemy came and sowed tares among the wheat and went his way. But when the grain had sprouted and produced a crop, then the tares also appeared. So the servants of the owner came and said to him, 'Sir, did you not sow good seeds in your field? How then does it have tares?' He said to them, 'An enemy has done this.' The servants said to him, 'Do you want us then to go and gather them up?' But he said, 'No, lest while you gather up the tares you also uproot the wheat with them. Let both grow together until the harvest, and at the time of the harvest I will say to the reapers, 'First gather together the tares and bind them in bundles to burn them, but gather the wheat into my barn.'" (Matt. 13:24–30)

This parable of our Lord reminds us that we are not to judge and that we must be patient with others. God is in charge, and He is comfortable with diversity in ways that may make us uncomfortable.

We should understand diversity as a sign of God's blessings and presence. In fact, Acts 2 describes a wide variety of people who come to follow Christ. Scripture teaches us in 1 Corinthians 12 that each person is welcomed and given a place within the Body of Christ: "There are diversities of gifts, but the same Spirit. . . . One and the same Spirit works all these things, distributing to each one individually as He wills" (vv. 4, 11). Jesus tells the sinful woman caught in adultery to "go and sin no more" (John 8:11); she is called to repent, but she is not excluded. Most importantly, the notion of diversity is found in Jesus' own words of the Great Commission: "Go therefore and make disciples of *all* the nations" (Matt. 28:19, italics mine).

Change has always been a part of the life of the Church, and positive changes breathe life and new perspectives into our Christian communities. We should never consider changing doctrine or the Church's historic teachings, but as my friend Fr. Theodore Dorrance likes to say, we *can* consider how we might change without changing what is unchangeable.

A Few Symptoms of Stagnation

» The parish does not have a meaningful impact on the community around it.

» If the church disappeared, no one would notice or protest its absence.

» Parishioners don't notice the world around them and can't understand its interests and needs.

» Parishioners come to believe that only what is important to them matters.

» Parishioners are delusional about themselves, their importance, and the world around them.

» Members care about the needs of a certain group, placing the interests of the few over those of the many. The parish shrinks slowly in size over time or stays about the same.

» Those who remain become more and more disfigured and lukewarm about Christ and the gospel.

» Parishioners notice that successive generations of their own kind leave the church, never to return—or are connected by only the thinnest of threads.

» Members of the community attend church out of routine instead of love for the Lord and their neighbors.

» Parishioners become consumers of what is sacred, but what is sacred does not reside in their hearts.

» The parish becomes insulated and parochial.

Review

Main Ideas

1. Resistance always accompanies any attempt to change.

2. Much resistance can be overcome through good communication and understanding.

3. Sabotage is a serious matter that must be dealt with immediately and forcefully.

4. Diversity is a positive element of parish life that leads to new ideas, growth, and gospel-centeredness.

Action Items

1. Gather and assess hard data, qualitative and quantitative, on your community, including attendance for worship, church school, and other events; demographics; engagement in spiritual practices and ministries; giving; and other important areas.

2. Discuss your findings with your leadership team, understanding that not every barrier can be removed or addressed at once.

    »   Identify one or two changes that would generate support and excitement.

    »   Where can you start removing barriers? What are some of the simple changes you can make to begin removing barriers?

3. Summarize your thoughts into a written statement.

For Contemplation

1. How do fear, internal resistance, and sabotage keep you from removing the barriers of your community?

2. How might you prayerfully approach pockets of resistance and people in positions of power to discuss the positive changes you'd like to see?

3. How can you begin a dialogue about the barriers you have identified?

4. What nonessentials have become sacred for your community, and in what ways have they replaced what is essential? Write in your journal about the culture of your parish. What do you notice?

PART III

Leadership Development
&
Creating a Parish Health Plan

CHAPTER SIX

Leadership

G ROWING UP IN A LARGE FAMILY as I did was a huge blessing. One characteristic of both my mother's and my father's families was their ability to carry on a conversation. It was not unusual for us to attend family gatherings that lasted late into the night. My family had a lot to say, and they needed time to say it.

But in this chapter I hope to buck this family trait and try to be brief. The truth is, there is so much to say on the topic of leadership that it would take volumes to say it all. And even then there would be more to say. My intent is to cover a few basic ideas that will provide you with a roadmap. However, anyone serious about reclaiming the Great Commission would be wise to take what little is offered here and add to it.

My Journey

I am inspired by what some call the art of leadership. I am also inspired by great leaders. I think this is true for most of us. In the Orthodox Church we celebrate a number of great leaders. For example, we have dedicated January 30 to recognizing three of the greatest leaders the Church has produced. The Feast of the Three Hierarchs acknowledges the incredible contributions of Ss. Basil the Great, John Chrysostom, and Gregory the Theologian.

At a certain point in my ministry, I realized that developing myself as a leader needed to be one of my life's goals. In my mind, this goal is not self-serving, nor is it an end in itself. Instead, authentic leadership is about serving others. It seems that St. Paul had this idea in mind when he wrote about the leadership of the Church in his Letter to the Ephesians:

> And He Himself gave some *to be* apostles, some prophets, some evangelists, and some pastors and teachers, for the equipping of the saints for the work of ministry, for the edifying of the body of Christ, till we all come to the unity of the faith and of the knowledge of the Son of God, to a perfect man, to the measure of the stature of the fullness of Christ; that we should no longer be children, tossed to and fro and carried about with every wind of doctrine, by the trickery of men, in the cunning craftiness of deceitful plotting, but, speaking the truth in love, may grow up in all things into Him who is the head—Christ—from whom the whole body, joined and knit together by what every joint supplies, according to the effective working by which every part does its share, causes growth of the body for the edifying of itself in love. (Eph. 4:11–16)

This passage reminds us of the centrality of leadership in the Body of Christ. Leadership equips the members of our communities; it edifies them, unites them in faith and knowledge, matures the church, and brings stability and direction. We can say that good leadership is what makes reclaiming the Great Commission possible.

Of course, we all bring to this journey differing sets of skills and abilities. I have come to recognize that my talents and limitations do not determine whether or not I can lead. The same is true for all of us. Rather, what matters is that we take this journey seriously, knowing that while we will grow, we will always discover more to learn and to improve as well as new horizons to behold. I plan to continue this journey for the rest of my life. It is a journey that has transformed me and, hopefully, those I have led.

I cannot say that I am a great leader, but I can say that I am learning to be a better one each day. A few years ago, a former parishioner wrote to me about her time at Saint Spyridon. She was very complimentary as she summarized her experiences during her time with us. However, as I read her letter, I couldn't help but cringe. Her descriptions of me at the time were not those of a developed leader. I remember thinking, "What was I thinking?" and "Why on earth would I have done that?" As the saying goes, hindsight is 20/20.

Looking through the rearview mirror at my decisions and actions as a leader is necessary, even though it is hard. I think about how I wish I had known back then what I know today. At the same time, I have enough experience to realize I will probably think the same way a few years from now. In the end, what this reflection has taught me is that growing as a leader is a constant process of refinement that must be undertaken with humility.

The journey is also something we share with others. This means I do not attempt to lead alone or to take on tasks that are beyond my abilities. To do so would be like trying to climb Mount Everest all by myself. Instead, a good leader gathers others to help lead.

A number of things take place in the parish that require skills I do not have. For example, I would make a terrible copy editor. I have no skill when it comes to editing, and my understanding of grammatical rules is rudimentary. My use of commas is based on whim and nothing more. Thankfully, this book had a good editor who carefully combed the manuscript, making changes and improvements.

In my parish, a number of people work on the development and compilation of our service books. They spend hours typesetting and editing the books so they can be used in the many services of the Orthodox Church throughout the year. As a leader, I have learned to seek and place into leadership those who have the right skills for the role.

A few years ago, our community decided it was time to add another priest. In a parish council meeting, one of the members said, "Father Evan, we need to find another priest just like you!"

"No," I replied. "It would be much better to find someone who has different skills and talents than I do."

This puzzled them until they thought about it some more. It is best for a community to have a leadership team with diverse skills and talents. And so my personal journey has included the growing commitment to find and develop leaders around me.

My journey has benefited from many things, but the main catalysts in my development have been my growing faith in Jesus Christ and the wisdom of other leaders. Most of what I have learned has come from my leadership team—from their example, experiences, writings, and willingness to work with me to help me grow. As I said previously, I no longer believe leaders are born. Now I know that leaders are made.

Lastly, to lead well I have learned that I must get acquainted with those I lead. This is not something I do out of obligation. It is not just another task. Rather, my Faith has taught me that a desire to know another human being is what love is all about. This is how I love God and my neighbor. Obviously, this desire cannot be contrived. It must come from the heart. Certainly, caring about those we lead models the way the greatest of leaders, Christ, led.

"I am the good shepherd. The good shepherd gives His life for the sheep. But a hireling, *he who is* not the shepherd, one who does not own the sheep, sees the wolf coming and leaves the sheep and flees; and the wolf catches the sheep and scatters them. The hireling flees because he is a hireling and does not care about the sheep. I am the good shepherd; and I know My *sheep,* and am known by My own. As the Father knows Me, even so I know the Father; and I lay down My life for the sheep. And other sheep I have which are not of this fold; them also I must bring, and they will hear My voice; and there will be one flock *and* one shepherd." (John 10:11–16)

I wish I could share with you all that I have learned and everything that has excited me about becoming a more developed leader, but that is not possible. And it is probably not needed. Remember that Jesus once promised the following:

"Ask, and it will be given to you; seek, and you will find; knock, and it will be opened to you. For everyone who asks receives, and he who seeks finds, and to him who knocks it will be opened. Or what man is there among you who, if his son asks for bread, will give him a stone? Or if he asks for a fish, will he give him a serpent? If you then . . . know how to give good gifts to your children, how much more will your Father who is in heaven give good things to those who ask Him!" (Matt. 7:7–11)

In other words, if you want to grow as a leader, you should not only ask but trust both God and those He has placed in your life to help you.

Leading Is the Leader's Job

As I wrote earlier, our personal journey toward becoming better leaders has a point: it is about serving others. I believe one of the greatest ways we can shape our parishes for the better is by leading them and not being led.

Many times I have failed to lead. Sometimes I have become too focused on the demands of the day. When this happens, I lose sight of what is important and concentrate only on what is in front of me. Other times I have failed to prayerfully think over what is going on around me before acting, becoming reactive instead of responsive.

Reactive behavior is often shortsighted and immediate; it is a knee-jerk and typically emotional response in which a leader does not consider the long-term implications of his or her actions. Responsive behavior is the opposite. It is thoughtful and reflective. A responsive leader considers both the short- and long-term impact of decisions and actions.

Reactive behavior can easily occur because of the complexity and pace of the challenges a leader faces. In some instances, I have hung back and operated as part of the pack, failing to see my opportunity to step forward and provide direction. Often, I have applied the wrong solution. For example, I have confused a tactical decision for a strategic one or a technical change for an adaptive one, in both cases failing to recognize which one was needed.[13]

---

13 The field of study that examines tactical decision-making versus strategic decision-making is rich and extremely beneficial. In addition to consulting the List of Resources on page 193, I highly recommend additional research and receive coaching on the subject. The same goes for the field of study that examines technical versus adaptive change. Developed leaders would do well to understand the differences and learn how to apply this knowledge in their community and decision-making.

Tactical versus Strategic Decision-making

Tactical decision making occurs in a short time frame. These are the concrete, definable plans we make and practices we follow. For example, we might decide that the reason for declining attendance in worship has to do with the time of the service. Thus, without thinking deeply or strategically about the issue, we make a tactical decision to move the service time from 9 AM to 10 AM.

In contrast, strategic decisions take into account a much longer view of our situation and context. Strategy making involves vision, mission, goals—even aspirations—and considers the general path we wish to take to achieve our objectives. In addressing the problem of declining attendance in worship, a strategic solution seeks to understand the deeper and more complex reasons behind the change. It steps back and away from the problem of declining attendance and attempts to develop a more robust and thoughtful response.

In the end, it may be that moving the time for the service is the correct decision. However, such a decision would be the result of a strategy that seeks to reengage people in worship. It is also likely that moving the service time is not all that we would do; rather, it would be only one component of our approach to enhancing parishioners' commitment to liturgical worship. Thus, a strategy that sought to bring more people into the transformational aspect of communal worship might also examine other aspects of worship, such as parishioners' level of spiritual formation, the physical space, and resources such as hymnals, language, and music.

Our tactical decisions should come out of an understanding of the overall strategy. They are the decisions that in small steps get us closer to the goals we set forth when making strategic decisions. The danger is that we mistakenly replace tactical thinking for strategic thinking or fail to develop or account for our strategy when determining our tactics.

For example, our bookstore began simply as a shelf in our original fellowship hall. Eventually, when we acquired our new location, it moved into its own space, and over time it has expanded further. Its leadership developed a new strategy that went beyond simply providing items for purchase. This new strategy was born out of their desire to support the vision and the mission of the parish to a greater extent.

Our vision statement reads, "An Orthodox community where people find transformation in Jesus Christ." We have several mission statements that are designed to support this vision, like muscles on a skeleton. These statements are gathered under four categories: worship, service, education, and community. Under the category of education the mission statement reads, "Providing resources to lead people to a deeper relationship with Jesus Christ."

As I mentioned above, ministry leaders are encouraged to work with and support the overall strategy of the parish as it is articulated in its vision and mission statements. It's easy to see how the bookstore ministry in its original form supported our vision and the education component of the mission statement by providing resources for purchase on Sunday. Working within this strategy of aligning with vision and mission, the leaders of the ministry made all sorts of tactical decisions, such as which books or icons to purchase, how much to sell them for, and when the bookstore should be open.

However, when we expanded and enhanced the strategy for the bookstore, a new set of tactical decisions needed to accompany it. I have to tell you that when the leaders of this ministry shared with me that they wanted to implement the vision and mission at a higher level, I was excited. They decided they wanted the bookstore to provide resources for conversation and growth that wouldn't be based on selling something. They didn't want parishioners to view the bookstore simply as a store.

Our first mission statement reads that our church is committed to worship "that is apostolic, biblical, and centered on community participation in prayer, music, and beauty." The bookstore leaders envisioned a ministry that would provide discussion and education about prayer, prayer space in one's home, the use of vigil lamps, and other spiritual resources. This, they believed, would help serve the parish by increasing people's engagement in worship.

Additionally, they wanted to help people outside our parish by providing them resources as well. This outreach addresses the fourth mission statement of the church's commitment to be a community "that welcomes all people into our spiritual family." They also addressed this fourth statement when they saw a need to provide more intimate spaces for people to gather and discuss their spiritual lives.

In the end, the ministry team needed to make a new set of tactical decisions to meet this new bookstore strategy. This led to an increase in the physical size of the store, equipment to allow for streaming of classes to those outside the parish, new intimate fellowship space, and a communication plan that would share these changes with others.

Technical and Adaptive Change

Adaptive and technical change are two very different things. We make technical changes when we understand the problem we face, have experience with it, and have expertise to guide us when making the change. Adaptive change requires us to learn new things and develop new skills—to adapt to an unfamiliar situation. A prime example for parishes today is learning how to minister in post-Christian America. We need to adapt to changing societal circumstances to share the gospel effectively. Our familiar canoes are the wrong tools to help us travel mountainous terrain.

To better understand adaptive change, we can think about the nearly universal problem facing churches of all types in all places— namely, the declining percentage of youth who remain in the Church.

When I was a child, my parish's youth group met every Sunday evening with great success. Additionally, even though I played many sports, none of the games were scheduled on Sunday morning. Sunday on the whole was a day that society reserved for church and family activities. So making it to church and then attending a youth event later in the day was in many ways easier than it is today.

Many of us, when facing the problem of youth who no longer attend church or youth events, or youth who leave the church when they hit their teens, turn toward solutions that are technical. We may simply try to do what worked in the past but place the event on a different day. If Sunday is now filled with sporting events, then getting a teen to church is simply a matter of scheduling the service during the week.

Now, while this may be true, it likely is not. Instead, the needed solutions are found in the adaptive realm. Retaining our youth is not a problem that can be solved with a technical solution. Instead, we need to seek solutions that are outside our current abilities and competencies. We are facing a new reality, and most youth ministers and advisers do not have ready answers. A spirit of innovation, discovery, and experimentation will likely result in greater success than a mere change in time and date or doing what worked in the past.

Orienting Our Leadership toward the Great Commission

In most cases, the chief cause of parish leaders' failure to lead has been our inability to see the forest for the trees—to stay focused on what is essential. I have found that a good starting point for getting ourselves oriented is the Great Commission.

The Great Commission is the reason the Church is here. It is our purpose. The Great Commission is not only about getting new people to join our communities—it is certainly much more than this. Notice that in the Bible Jesus asks not only that we go forth to baptize all nations but that we "[teach] them to observe all things that I have commanded you" (Matt. 28:20). This means that reclaiming the Great Commission is also about ensuring that our community members live an authentic and vibrant life in Christ.

Honestly, though, in many communities we are struggling. We are not fulfilling the Great Commission, and we are not helping people connect and commit deeply to Jesus. This is the fault of poor leadership. So how can our communities change? What will bring about not only the discussion but the implementation of the ideas presented in this book? Simply put, change will only come when our leaders determine to make it happen. It will come when leaders like you have the courage to do what you know is right despite the risks and challenges that face us. We need leaders like Joseph of Arimathea: "a prominent council member, who was himself waiting for the kingdom of God, coming and taking courage, went in to Pilate and asked for the body of Jesus" (Mark 15:43). Joseph had enough courage to do the right thing—to lead.

To bring about positive changes, leaders like you will need to take on the essential and delicate job of leading your community into reclaiming the Great Commission. You will need courage, and you will need integrity, but you will also need to give this endeavor your constant attention.

As I mentioned before, the times I have failed to lead well are innumerable. One instance occurred during the writing of this book. A ministry that had for years operated well had plateaued and declined. In many ways, it was falling apart. I had failed to notice, and even when certain symptoms came to my attention, I ignored them and brushed them off. It wasn't until things reached a level of dysfunction and rebellion that I woke up.

Leading well is like gardening well. Yes, we have to prepare the soil, plant, and water, but we also need to tend to the vegetables in the garden constantly. In my case, I had become overly concerned about the tomatoes and the peppers while ignoring the cucumbers. Of course, all is not lost. Good leadership and a renewed focus on this ministry led to an eventual resurgence.

Remember, the change we want to see in our parishes begins in us; developing ourselves will have to come first. The change in our own hearts is what makes it possible to develop others.

To this day, I remain enthusiastic about the gospel, and my childhood excitement has not diminished. As hard as leading can be, the effort is still worthwhile, and I am hopeful that more and more of the conversations we have within the Church at large will focus on leadership and its role in leading positive change.

The Basics of Developed Leadership

Part One: Vision and Mission Setting

The first task of a leader is to set the vision and mission of the community. Like Moses, who led Israel out of captivity, today's leader provides the parish its direction and its identity. This is exactly what God did when He announced through an angel to Joseph that Jesus was going to be born *to save us from our sins* (Matt. 1:21). God communicated the purpose of Jesus' mission. In a similar way, a good leader also provides guidance to the community and gives it its purpose. When this purpose is clearly communicated, the leader can then go about organizing the community to accomplish the vision and mission. I will briefly define these two essentials here.

A vision statement[14] expresses your core values and inspires the

---

14   The terms *vision statement* and *mission statement* can be confusing, and many times they are used interchangeably. Not long ago I gave a presentation on vision and mission statements that ended with a complete refutation by a successful businessman. He argued passionately that I was using the terms wrongly—that what I defined as a vision statement was actually a mission statement, and vice

people in your community. Vision statements are aspirational—they provide us an opportunity to put our dreams on paper. Through developing vision statements, we capture the hearts and imaginations of the community to go beyond what it currently is and has already accomplished. We also set ourselves on a path and a journey that leads us forward positively—a journey that will never end.

As noted earlier, Saint Spyridon's vision statement is, "An Orthodox community where people find transformation in Jesus Christ." This statement provides people a glimpse of our core values and aspirations: we are Orthodox Christians, we are building a strong community, we focus on the needs of people, we aspire to transformation, and it all happens in Jesus. It is also a vision that we do not expect ever to realize completely.

A mission statement of a parish supports the vision in a more concrete way. Mission statements provide some of the muscles on the skeleton. In general, they tell the story and communicate to your community and those outside *how* you intend to go about accomplishing your vision. Here are the mission statements of Saint Spyridon:

As a church we are committed to:

WORSHIP that is apostolic, biblical, and centered on community participation in prayer, music, and beauty.

SERVICE that ministers through evangelization, philanthropy, pastoral care, and stewardship.

EDUCATION that provides resources to lead people to a deeper relationship with Jesus Christ.

COMMUNITY that welcomes all people into our spiritual family.

---

versa. Ironically, in the same presentation, another participant who worked in the field of organizational management sided with me! To be honest, I think we can use these terms interchangeably without affecting what these statements do for our parishes.

On the whole, vision and mission statements encapsulate the hopes, goals, and values you have developed as a parish. Their adoption is crucial. They become the standards and the guiding light by which you measure every aspect of the life of the parish.

At Saint Spyridon we have a number of ministries. Some are rather complicated, and others are fairly straightforward and simple. Yet each of them plays a part in advancing the vision and mission of the church. For example, we have a small group ministry for baking the offering bread brought to each Liturgy. Even this group of bakers serves the vision and mission. In baking bread for the Liturgy, they participate in the process of building an Orthodox community. In truth, the holy task of baking and bringing bread is an act of transformation and a connection with the life and sacrifice of Jesus Christ.

In meeting with the leaders and members of this ministry, I have spoken to them about how their work supports the worship of our community. We have discussed bread baking as an act of service. In turn, bakers have shared how making the bread in their homes has provided an opportunity to learn more about their Faith and to share it with their children and friends. Additionally, we encourage the individual bakers to meet from time to time with one another and share tips on baking, forming social connections that lead to the building of relationships.

Another ministry of the parish is the myrrh-bearers, a prayer ministry that has committed itself to the daily office of intercessory prayer. Each day this group of faithful community members prays for each person who has entrusted them with a prayer request. Additionally, participants of this ministry are scheduled to pray in each Divine Liturgy. They arrive early, when one of the members of the baking ministry brings the offering bread.

During the service of oblation before the Liturgy, the clergy prepare the elements of the bread and wine. As the bread that will become the Body is placed on the paten (a small plate that holds the bread), individual names and sometimes specific requests are lifted up in prayer. The myrrh-bearers participate in this sacred task alongside the clergy, offering the prayer requests and the names that have been submitted to them. Like the baking ministry, this small group ministry supports the vision and mission statements of the parish.

Setting your vision and mission statements provides leaders with the opportunity to express your core values and the guiding principles by which you are operating. These words will then both guide your members (those inside the church) and express to the community at large (those outside) who you are.

In the end, vision and mission statements tell the people what you are about and, to a degree, how you plan to implement your ideas. I strongly suggest that these statements support the multidimensional definition and concepts of parish health from chapter 3.

Steps for Creating Your Parish's Vision and Mission

To establish your vision and mission, you, the leaders, must ask and answer several fundamental questions of yourselves. I recommend that you go about this in two steps.

STEP 1

I encourage you first to pray, be silent, and open your heart to the Holy Spirit so you can step away from the demands of the day, think outside the box, and do some soul searching. Start by writing down your answers to these questions:

» When did I become a Christian and why?

» Why am I a disciple of Christ, and what does my faith in Jesus Christ and the gospel invite me to consider?

» Why did I become a priest/parish council member/ministry leader/Christian?

» How am I working or not working toward the Great Commission?

» What is important to me, how do I spend my time, and what drives me?

Let me reiterate how vital it is to get outside what you know and what you have inherited. It may help you to think, "If I were starting this community from scratch, what would I do? What would I emphasize?" You need to think deeply about these questions, laboring over your answers while pushing yourself to get out of your typical way of thinking and the ditches you may be living in. Remember that even Moses spent forty days up on Mount Sinai before he came down and articulated God's plan to His people.

I remember the first time I sat down to craft the vision and mission of Saint Spyridon. My mentor suggested that I craft them first on my own. He wanted me to get in touch with myself and my core beliefs. This work on the vision and mission he encouraged me to do thoughtfully, prayerfully, and over time.

The exercise was both illuminating and energizing. After I crafted a vision and mission, my mentor encouraged me to work with a small group to refine my ideas. (In the next chapter I outline this process in more detail.) This small group, the Parish Health Team, was also invested in the development of the vision and mission of the community.

The key point here is that I did not go into those discussions with others unprepared. I was ready to articulate my vision and mission statements and the reasons behind them.

STEP 2

In this next step, ask and answer these fundamental questions related to your community's identity:

» What is our purpose?

» Why are we here?

» What opportunities has God given us?

Let me stress that the process of asking and answering these questions is the responsibility of the leader and then, by extension, the rest of the leadership. Leaders are the ones who need to set the direction for the parish. Of course, what we want to avoid is ruling by decree like an autocrat or developing things in such a way that the people we lead feel left out and left behind.

Don't forget in responding to these questions to make an effort to avoid simply applying an answer you have inherited. Many of our communities today seem to be operating under a vision and mission that was handed down to them from the past. They are trapped by a history that didn't or couldn't make room for the Great Commission.

A decade ago, I was asked to consult with a priest who had been assigned to a parish that was over a hundred years old. Needless to say, he was inheriting a community with a long and established history. Right away, he noticed that this parish's history was both an asset and a barrier. The community in many ways had been wrapped up in its past and trapped by it.

The initial founding of the parish occurred when a group of immigrants moved to an area in the western part of the United States. These immigrants came west to work in the mines, and they brought with them their families and their Orthodox Faith. As with many mining towns in the West, mining and immigration eventually petered out. In its place, these mountain towns have attracted new residents and new industries. Many of the cultural and linguistic traditions of these earlier years have died out.

However, this community had become increasingly focused on remembering and honoring its history, resulting in a drastic loss in membership and a calcification of ideas and activities. Old and irrelevant ministries and associations still retained places of prominence and determined the rhythm and life of the parish. It was obvious that changes were necessary, and a respectful but directed break with this parish's history would need to occur if it was to survive and thrive in the twenty-first century.

Part Two: Identifying Our Purpose

After answering the questions in Part One, leaders must ask themselves, "Where is my community going right now? What is our current direction and purpose?" What we are trying to assess is just how close your community is to the vision and mission you have developed in the previous step.

It is not unusual to notice a disconnect at this stage. You may find that your parish is not pointed toward your vision and mission and that you are not on track to reclaim the Great Commission. In some cases, you may discover that no real vision or mission exists for your community. Remember my description of why defining parish health is important in chapter 3. My cousin's former parish was misguided in its direction, and the leadership lacked clarity of purpose. If this is the case in your community, you as a leader need to understand that this process of asking and answering questions must broaden.

When a disconnect exists between vision and current reality, you will need to lead your parish through the same process you have completed. This time, however, the leader needs to supply steady guidance and encouragement to those being led in order to avoid getting sidetracked and/or garnering too much resistance.

For example, when Christ shared with His own disciples the purpose of His life, they resisted Him:

> From that time Jesus began to show to His disciples that He must go to Jerusalem, and suffer many things from the elders and chief priests and scribes, and be killed, and be raised the third day. Then Peter took Him aside and began to rebuke Him, saying, "Far be it from You, Lord; this shall not happen to You!" But He turned and said to Peter, "Get behind Me, Satan! You are an offense to Me, for you are not mindful of the things of God, but the things of men." Then Jesus said to His disciples, "If anyone desires to come after Me, let him deny himself, and take up his cross, and follow Me. For whoever desires to save his life will lose it, but whoever loses his life for My sake will find it. For what profit is it to a man if he gains the whole world, and loses his own soul? Or what will a man give in exchange for his soul? For the Son of Man will come in the glory of His Father with His angels, and then He will reward each according to his works." (Matt. 16:21–27; see also Luke 9:43–50)

Not only did Jesus meet resistance from those He led, but they suggested alternative destinations. Importantly, Christ did not yield to the group. Rather, He remained clear about His purpose and worked tirelessly to bring His disciples to the same understanding He had about His true purpose and identity.

As in the case of the disciples, so also in our parishes, agreement and cooperation do not happen easily or quickly. Therefore, leaders need to move softly but firmly over time as they share their discoveries. With a clear and gradual approach, they will be able to build broader support within the community for this new understanding. (We will discuss communication later in this chapter.)

In chapters 4 and 5, we examined the barriers that often fill in the gap between the vision and mission we want and the disfigured identity we currently have. Not only do leaders need to address these barriers, but they need to implement the positive changes already discussed, especially regarding parish health. To do this you will need to answer yet another question: "How do we get to where we want to go?"

Part Three: Strategic Planning

To answer the question, "How do we get where we want to go?" leaders organize their communities around a plan. I mentioned earlier the purpose of a strategic plan. This is one of your key resources to help get your community moving in the right direction.

At the most basic level, I understand the process of strategic planning as disciplined and thoughtful. It is not something we do in an ad hoc manner. Rather, in developing your plan, it is important that you have a structure that encourages honest dialogue, listening with humility, and a drive to better understand yourselves and your community.

I also believe that it is the leaders in your community who must initiate this process and see it through. In order to successfully develop your plan, you will also need to seek help from within the parish and from outside it.

The objective of strategic planning is to develop the structure that will support your vision and mission as well as the answers to the questions you have asked yourself in Part One and Part Two of the Basics of Developed Leadership. With your strategic plan in place, you know what to focus on, and so does your community. The plan you develop helps you to guide who will be doing what and when it will happen. Importantly, with a strategic plan in place, you can more effectively deploy your limited resources to accomplish your vision, mission, and goals.

For example, in our most recent strategic plan our parish set the long-range goal of strengthening the fabric of our community through deepening the community's relationship with the Holy Trinity and with one another. To accomplish this, we developed a number of SMART goals (Specific, Measurable, Action-oriented, Realistic, and Timely). SMART goal number one states that in the next two years, we will increase and grow the liturgical life of the parish by providing more ways for people to engage in worship. We will accomplish this by adding services, acquiring digital service books, and providing classes on worship. These tasks were assigned to specific people and ministry leaders in the parish. We also developed other SMART goals to support this long-range strategic goal.

Keep in mind that not everything you want to accomplish will be possible. However, the plan will keep you on track and pointed toward the Great Commission. When this remains your focus, additional positive aspects of your vision and mission can be incorporated over time. I suggest that you investigate the field of strategic planning further before initiating this process.

Part Four: Communicating

What comes next is the opportunity to share more broadly and explicitly the vision and mission as well as the strategic plan that has been developed to support it. After answering the question of how to get where you want to go, leaders like yourself take on the responsibility of communicating all this with your parish. You stay in touch with your members, raising their level of excitement, motivation, ability, and drive to accomplish what the community has set out to do.

I know from experience that simply placing my ideas on paper is not enough. The process of communicating and achieving results is much more delicate and complicated. This means you need to build support and bring people together. You need to work on changing the culture of your parish in a positive way. Inventory the talents of those already in your community, and encourage them to use their gifts, which can assist and further your plans.

Getting your parish to understand and support the strategic plan requires leaders to share and discuss the plan in every setting. Not only did we incorporate Saint Spyridon's leaders when drafting the strategic plan, we held meetings with the community at large to discuss it. We printed copies of the plan, handed them to every member, and brought it to our parish's general assembly. The vision and mission statements appear on our website and in our weekly Sunday announcements, our newsletter, and other communications. We discuss them in every team, committee, and ministry meeting, and I discuss them one on one with individual parishioners.

Leaders need to understand that for the process of transformation to occur, the culture and identity of the parish must be shepherded through stages of development. Culture and identity must develop in such a way that they will support the vision and mission. This is why a leader moves delicately but consistently and with patience, understanding that this process is a multiyear effort. And for our efforts to bear fruit, the process must be undergirded by humble, fervent prayer. We are not building a corporation; we are, with God's help, building up the Body of Christ in our parishes: "Unless the Lord builds the house, / Those who build it labor in vain" (Ps. 126/127:1 OSB).

A healthy leader knows just how important it is to build not only a relationship with God but relationships within the community. In doing so a leader comes to understand people's abilities, interests, and much more. These conversations inform you as leaders and also inform those you lead, ensuring that communication within the parish is two-way, open, and honest.

Sharing the community's vision and mission is an important component in your conversations with members. One outcome of these conversations is the building of trust at all levels because of leadership involvement and transparency. Additionally, as trust builds, you come to understand who is ready for a greater level of responsibility within the community. Leaders then commission, deploy, and entrust these people with key elements of the plans.

Of course, trusting others and empowering them does not mean you fail to stay engaged. Rather, you stay involved at an appropriate level, guiding the overall direction without constantly looking over people's shoulders and controlling their actions and decisions.

As a side note, it is good to know that in recruiting and deploying other leaders, a developed leader needs to sort out the balance between two factors: risk and control. If we imagine a teeter-totter with risk on one end and control on the other, a poor leader would favor only one. Thus, he or she may choose to eliminate risk by elevating the amount of control he or she has over others and the ministry, which is unhealthy and stifling.

On the other hand, the leader may choose to lead in a totally hands-off way and as a result have little to no control over what occurs. This elevates the risk that something destructive or dangerous will take place in the community. Good leaders balance risk and control by developing a healthy and thorough understanding of the vision and mission of the parish in those they lead and in their coleaders.

One example of this balance in my parish is the St. Nicodemus burial society, which comes alongside families who have lost a loved one and supports them from the time of death through the memorial. As the ministry was being formed, I met with its leadership frequently and spent many hours reviewing and discussing with them the parish's vision and mission, along with our strategic plan and its goals and organizational structure.

Eventually, I asked the coleaders to develop a vision and mission that aligned with the parish's goals and that would work synergistically with them. This process allowed us to reach a balance between control and risk. It also helped the coleaders to do the same with those who became participants in the ministry. Following this process with all our ministries helps us work toward the goal of developing others with skills unlike our own. It also keeps us on track and prevents us from losing sight of our goals.

Part Five: Execution

This final step of aligning the parish under a vision, mission, and strategic plan is not easy. It is also something that I learned cannot be left to chance or placed on autopilot. Instead, this task requires me, as well as the rest of our leaders, to take regular stock of where we are with regard to the Great Commission and to work toward the implementation of our ideas. And because I don't want to lose my way, I have found that I have to examine my own heart and mind regularly. I have to ask myself those fundamental questions I listed in Part One again and again. This is an ongoing process if a parish is to avoid stagnation.

In the end, execution of our vision, mission, and plans is key. If you do all that is mentioned here but fail to take the actions listed in your plan and carry them through, then ultimately the change you hope to see will not be realized. Leadership is about guiding the implementation of the plan, developing the talent within the community, and keeping your hand on the plow in order to see things through.

I remember speaking with a bishop who oversees a large number of churches about many of the things I have written in this book. "Father Evan," he asked me, "what do you think would keep me and the communities under my oversight from successfully reclaiming the Great Commission?"

My reply was simple: "A failure to execute over time." Staying on task helps us avoid the fate of Lot's wife: "But his wife looked back behind him, and she became a pillar of salt" (Gen. 19:26).

A Few Ideas on Developing as a Leader

Here I'd like to devote a few paragraphs to encouraging you and providing you with some insights on enhancing your leadership skills.

Let me begin by saying that many resources are available to you—people, books, classes, seminars, retreats, videos, and podcasts that will help anyone who is interested to learn more about the art of leadership. Taking advantage of these resources is how I have developed and how I continue to learn. Let me emphasize, however, that the initiative must come from within. And if it is there, if the desire to develop exists, then the skies are the limit. You will be amazed at how many people are willing to help you and how many resources are right at your fingertips. So don't be discouraged!

Second, in order to grow, you will have to get to know yourself better. You need to know who you are, your values, and your principles. Without this knowledge, it is hard to be an effective leader. In a way, the answers to these questions help us understand how we want to operate, what our nonnegotiables are, and the signposts that will guide us while we lead. In this process of knowing ourselves, we grow our own emotional intelligence—an area of exploration I highly encourage you to examine—by knowing our strengths and our weaknesses and how to work with others. We come to understand better our own abilities and aspirations. We answer the questions, "Where do I want to go, and how do I want to spend my time?"

Next, we should work on becoming better communicators. I have realized that my communication style is not yet perfect. I am learning that communicating humbly and from the heart is essential, as well as communicating with consistency, clarity, and simplicity. I have learned that when I do not articulate myself clearly, parishioners misunderstand or make assumptions about what I mean. I have also learned that while I don't need to be an exemplary orator, I do need to engage those around me so that I can inspire them, ignite their flame for the Great Commission, and encourage them that the journey we are on is worth all this effort.

Hopefully, the way we have discussed leadership here does not lead us to forget that we are first and foremost followers of Jesus.

> Therefore we also, since we are surrounded by so great a cloud of witnesses, let us lay aside every weight, and the sin which so easily ensnares *us*, and let us run with endurance the race that is set before us, looking unto Jesus, the author and finisher of *our* faith, who for the joy that was set before Him endured the cross, despising the shame, and has sat down at the right hand of the throne of God. (Heb. 12:1–2)

The model of Jesus is the model of Christian leadership. And so we enter into the personal arena of growth with Jesus, through a growing relationship with Him. This means we not only study and imitate His life, but we foster a rich relationship with Him through prayer—prayer that opens to us the possibility of a relationship with the Father and the Holy Spirit.

We must also face the need to accept the risks and responsibility that come with leading and achieving the results we seek. If we are going to lead well, we have to realize that not everything will go as planned. Leading well also means that we must accept responsibility when things fall apart. Thankfully, well-intentioned people will understand that failures occur, and when we are honest and take responsibility, they are accepting and supportive.

At the same time, those we lead have the right to expect results. We should also have an internal measuring stick, based on our own core values, that inspires us to achieve our goals. We use as our standard the answers to the questions we asked ourselves earlier in the process.

In the end, becoming a better leader is about stretching ourselves. It is about getting out of our comfort zone. It is about adopting the mindset found in these words of the great Apostle Paul:

Not that I have already attained, or am already perfected; but I press on, that I may lay hold of that for which Christ Jesus has also laid hold of me. Brethren, I do not count myself to have apprehended; but one thing *I do*, forgetting those things which are behind and reaching forward to those things which are ahead, I press toward the goal for the prize of the upward call of God in Christ Jesus. (Phil. 3:12–14)

Review

Main Ideas

1. We need to take this journey seriously and with humility.

2. The change we want to see in our parishes begins with our leaders and a team of committed Christians.

3. We need to answer the questions, "Why are we here? What are we trying to achieve?"

4. Leaders move softly and firmly, and over time they build support for their direction within their community.

5. Communication at every stage and at all times is key.

6. Change will not be realized without proper execution.

Action Items

1. Identify and examine what leadership styles and gifts are missing in you and your leadership team. Constantly seek to improve both.

2.   Expand your team to fill in the gaps you have identified.

3.   Identify roles and areas of oversight for your team as you move forward.

4.   Invest in a leadership program for your parish.

For Contemplation

1.   Is there a danger in becoming too structured in your approach?

2.   How do you identify whether the virtue of humility is missing in your leadership team?

3.   How will you keep the vision and mission of your community front and center?

4.   How can you work toward keeping your team and your parish unified and focused on your goals?

CHAPTER SEVEN

Creating a Parish Health Plan

For which of you, intending to build a tower, does not sit down first and count the cost, whether he has *enough* to finish *it*—lest, after he has laid the foundation, and is not able to finish, all who see *it* begin to mock him, saying, "This man began to build and was not able to finish"?

— Luke 14:28–30

THIS PARABLE OF THE TOWER is a sobering one. As we come to the last chapter of this book, Jesus' words remind me that learning about various concepts is useless without applying them. The parable also reminds me that before I set out on something as important as reclaiming the Great Commission, I should "sit down first and count the cost."

With this in mind, let's turn our attention to the process of creating a Parish Health Plan. A Parish Health Plan makes it possible to reclaim the Great Commission by focusing your community on the four components of parish health described in chapter 3, helping you to remove the barriers described in chapters 4 and 5, and developing the leaders described in chapter 6. In other words, a Parish Health Plan helps us to finish the job.

As in the previous chapters, my explanation of a Parish Health Plan cannot be exhaustive. I recognize that readers can always find ways to improve on what I've offered by applying newly acquired knowledge and experience. What I provide here is a roadmap, and we shouldn't view it rigidly. Instead, I want to encourage you to develop your own path forward, using the format here in such a way that you can incorporate your own knowledge and your community's unique resources, opportunities, and challenges.

Keep in mind that developing your plan requires you to act with a measure of skill and artistry. Think of yourself as a chef or a great artist at work on a masterpiece. As you move forward, you will have to make some decisions without having a clear answer in view. When an adaptive change is needed, you will have to use your intuition or love of exploration. At other times you will know the path to take, because a technical change is required. Either way, it is okay to experiment, learn, and readjust as you go, praying for the Holy Spirit's guidance. No one should expect changes to unfold mechanically or predictably.

I should also note that while the plan I am offering is linear in its progression, the process of reclaiming the Great Commission will not look like a straight line. As we work together in our communities, we will experience both ups and downs, setbacks and successes. But the general progression will be positive over time, so don't become discouraged when things get tough.

Phase 1: Form a Leadership Team

1. The first step in your Parish Health Plan is to form a Parish Health Team (PHT). This team should be commissioned by your community's clergy, parish board, and other governing

bodies—your established leadership structure, which I will refer to from now on as "governing bodies." It should take about a month to assemble this team.

» The governing bodies need to think carefully about the people involved. You need to recruit a team that is talented, committed, diverse, and includes the right mix of people. Do not pick just anyone!

» The team should be made up of engaged, active, knowledgeable people who are key leaders within your community. I strongly suggest that the core of this group include selected members from your clergy, key board members, key ministry leaders, and other committed and engaged community members.

» The time commitment for PHT members is a minimum of three years, and the team should not exceed twelve members. Too large a group leads to an unwieldy decision-making process.

2. The next step in your Parish Health Plan focuses on developing the team and becoming unified.

» For your plan to be successful, each PHT member must be committed and willing to contribute. Members cannot be mere placeholders or figureheads.

» The PHT should establish a conversation covenant using the principles of ORCA (open, respectful, curious, and accountable; see p. 101), a governance structure for decision-making and defining roles and responsibilities, a pace for the timing of their work, and general expectations.

◊ Governance structure: The PHT needs to determine how it wants to organize itself. I suggest that the team select a chair, someone to lead the team and help guide the overall Parish Health Plan. The team should then decide whether to elect officers such as a cochair, secretary, and others. The group should also determine how they will run meetings, vote, and make decisions.

◊ Pace: The PHT needs to agree to the frequency of meetings and determine a timeline for their work.

◊ General expectations: The PHT should set expectations for its operation. For example, members may decide that all reports and supporting information should be submitted forty-eight hours prior to a scheduled meeting and that meetings will not exceed ninety minutes in length.

» The PHT should also spend time discussing roles and responsibilities with the established governing bodies. It should be clear to all parties what the PHT's job is and how the team will go about accomplishing it. The governing bodies in the community must provide clear support for the work the PHT is doing. Support means that:

◊ The governing bodies and PHT are on the same page, encourage each other, and speak with the same voice.

◊ Clear and robust two-way communication occurs frequently between the governing bodies and the PHT.

◊ Active listening among all parties is encouraged to ensure that everyone is being heard and is on board with the plan. We can't make decisions by decree.

» During this stage it is helpful for the team to inventory its abilities, strengths, experiences, and weaknesses. Some self-work should be introduced, especially in the area of leadership, and this work should carry on throughout the process. Parish leaders should seek outside expertise in this area. A specialist can help the team with building its leadership skills, and the PHT can assign reading and make use of seminars, retreats, and workshops.

» It is essential that the team come together—that they coalesce—to understand and support everything a journey toward parish health entails. This process cannot be rushed or based on a forced or false unity. Instead, the team should follow the conversation covenant to ensure that all members are in an open and honest dialogue of discovery. Whoever is leading the PHT should assist in this by avoiding the temptation to become partisan or to take sides and force an agreement without everyone being totally on board.

» It is essential that the team speak with one voice. Individual members of the PHT must not undermine the team's work by speaking against or in opposition to the PHT with parishioners. This does not mean rigorous debate and disagreements should not take place within the PHT's deliberations. In fact, these differing opinions and perspectives are beneficial and help us to craft a more robust vision, mission, and plan. However, the goal is unity. The PHT needs to come to a place in which every member of the team has bought into what they are attempting to accomplish. This means that once the team has set a course, members of the PHT must be willing to support the team over their individual objectives or perspectives. Doing otherwise is extremely counterproductive and corrosive.

3. The next step in the Parish Health Plan can take many months to accomplish. The PHT will need to spend disciplined time together, practicing the concepts in this book and those found elsewhere that will assist the community in reclaiming the Great Commission.

    » Review and discuss the story of Fr. Elias found in the Introduction and consider how it relates to your community.

    » Consider and discuss how each member's personal journey toward reclaiming the Great Commission is essential to the community's transformation.

    » Establish a historical narrative for your community. It is important that the PHT gather accurate information about the formation, growth, and general story of the parish. It is important to understand who the parish has been, what its focus was and is today, and what milestones have occurred over time.

» Review and discuss the Five Essentials in the journey of reclaiming the Great Commission: regaining our sight, remembering our lifesaving mission, pruning, building bridges and not barriers, and developing a sense of urgency.

» Review and discuss the four concepts of parish health and how they might be implemented in the community's life: a commitment to Christ and the gospel (orthodoxia), a commitment to connecting Christ and the gospel to my daily life (orthopraxia), a commitment to relationship building and forming a spiritual family (koinonia), and a commitment to operational excellence (politea).

» Review and discuss the five barriers to parish health: undeveloped leadership, leaders without a plan, unbalanced identity, resistance and sabotage, and stagnation. The PHT members should also discuss any additional barriers that exist within the community.

» Review and discuss the key concepts of developed leaders (vision and mission setting, identifying our purpose, strategic planning, and communicating) and consider first how PHT members can improve as leaders and then how to build a leadership development plan for the community.

4. Next, the PHT outlines its work and develops a timeline for it. This step takes about two months to accomplish. To some degree, the timeline offered in this chapter provides a roadmap for the one the PHT is forming. The timeline for your community's PHT depends on your community's goals, internal sense of urgency, the pace the team has agreed to, and the level of engagement from PHT members.

» The PHT should develop a comprehensive communication plan for the entire community. This plan details how the PHT will dialogue with the parish. The focus of the plan is on consistent, clear, and concise updates that allow for two-way communication. These updates should be added to the timeline the team is developing.

» Some notes on support and communication:

◊ Support within the community depends on the PHT. Members need to work in a cohesive way and speak with one voice.

◊ Support will increase through effective communication with the community.

◊ Support depends on the PHT listening actively and attentively to parishioners and answering their questions and concerns. This will help minimize the amount of resistance to the positive changes that will be implemented.

◊ Communication requires careful planning and should include various avenues: sermons, town-hall-style gatherings, one-on-one conversations, workshops, retreats, and printed materials.

◊ Communication requires people who have developed good communication skills—people who can articulate clearly and consistently and paint the picture of your Parish Health Plan.

5. The last step in Phase 1 of the PHT's work is to prepare the community at large for change. The PHT needs to organize meetings in which it will present, educate, and discuss at a higher level the basics of parish health found in this book, the timeline the team has developed, and the Parish Health Plan—the work that the PHT will be doing. The team should take great care in communicating with parish members in order to answer questions, garner support, and help people understand the process. This part of the plan can take up to three months to complete.

Phase 2: Strategic Planning

In Phase 2 of your Parish Health Plan, the PHT develops a strategic plan for the community. This step can be completed in about six to eight months if your team is focused and works consistently.

However, it typically takes much longer. I highly recommend hiring someone trained in developing a strategic plan. For our first pass at a plan, Saint Spyridon brought in two outside specialists who helped us. Their involvement was critical.

» Please note that I am not providing a detailed discussion of strategic planning in this book. Rather, I have listed this step where I think it belongs in a Parish Health Plan. It is up to your PHT to account for the development of this plan and to gather the resources needed to accomplish it.

» The process of developing a strategic plan is key to your implementation of the concepts in this book. It is essential that your strategic plan includes principles you have learned here and elsewhere that can help you reclaim the Great Commission. At the same time, you must realize you will not be able to include all that you have learned in the first version of your first plan, or even in subsequent versions in the years to come. Although your parish's vision and mission will remain constant, certain elements of your strategic plan should be updated every few years and/or could be tweaked as you move forward and as circumstances change. This review can happen quarterly or annually.

» To reclaim the Great Commission, your parish needs to put into place what you can manage now, knowing that as you move forward and revise and update your strategic plan, additional elements of parish health will be included. In time, an increasing number of the concepts related to reclaiming the Great Commission will become part of your community's culture and identity. Don't forget to communicate regularly with your parish during this process.

» A special word on vision and mission statements:

◊ Please refer to the section "The Basics of Developed Leadership, Part One: Vision and Mission Setting" in chapter 6 (p. 160).

◊ Remember that the purpose of vision and mission statements is to express your core values and guiding principles, as well as how you plan to implement your ideas, to your members inside the church and also to the community at large—those outside.

◊ These statements also encapsulate your hopes and goals for your parish's future.

◊ I strongly suggest that these vision and mission statements support the multidimensional definition and concepts for parish health offered in this book.

Phase 3: Sharing the Plan

1. Step one in Phase 3 is sharing your strategic plan with the community. While sharing likely began earlier, in Phase 3 you work diligently at sharing and gaining support for the plan at every level within the parish. This work should take about two months, but it is an ongoing task for the PHT, for every leader in your community, and to a degree for every member of the parish. Your goal is to create a shared understanding that permeates all you do in the community.

2. In step two, the PHT works alongside and with the established leaders, structures, and stakeholders within the community to see that the strategic plan is implemented. Implementation should occur at the broadest and also at the most minuscule levels. You are attempting to build congruency and focus throughout the parish. The timeframe for this is, like step one, initially about two months of intensive work, but it is also ongoing.

3. In both steps one and two of Phase 3, the PHT stays engaged along with the other leaders in your community to ensure that your reclaiming of the Great Commission does not fade from focus. For many communities, the key failure point is just this—the inability to keep their focus on this task over the long term.

Phase 4: Renewal and Retooling

Phase 4 of your Parish Health Plan is an in-depth annual review by the PHT that looks at the community's progress toward reclaiming the Great Commission. This review is something that should start one year after the initial implementation of the parish's strategic plan. At the end of this review, the PHT should generate a report of action steps and share it with the governing bodies.

In my view, every community should have a Parish Health Team that works indefinitely on the elements of parish health. We can always find opportunities to improve our health. A PHT should constantly work toward pruning, fertilizing, planting, and innovating. This effort will help us avoid getting stuck or regressing into an endless cycle that is neither life-giving nor helpful.

The membership of the PHT should change over time, with some members continuing in their work and new members joining every year for a three-year term. It is possible that the PHT could be incorporated into the governing structures of the community. However, it should be noted that reclaiming the Great Commission should not become a subset of the parish's life. Rather, it should become the heartbeat of the parish. This shift in emphasis occurs when the components of parish health are increasingly prevalent in the day-to-day life of the parish. It happens when the barriers we have described and the ones you have identified are weakened, and the leadership of your community commits to its continued development. This continued development should be an ongoing focus of your PHT and the strategic plan. It is also a continual part of the PHT's work.

Final Thoughts on a Parish Health Plan

As I noted in the beginning of this chapter, this outline of steps is just a roadmap. This chapter does not account for every possible path to a successful Parish Health Plan. At the same time, if a community decides to employ the steps in this chapter as is, I believe great strides toward parish health and reclaiming the Great Commission are possible. Of course, what we do with what we learn is key. In my spiritual walk, I am often encouraged and challenged by the words of Christ, who told His disciples:

> But why do you call Me "Lord, Lord," and not do the things which I say? Whoever comes to Me, and hears My sayings and does them, I will show you whom he is like: He is like a man building a house, who dug deep and laid the foundation on the rock. And when the flood arose, the stream beat vehemently against that house, and could not shake it, for it was founded on the rock. But he who heard and did nothing is like a man who built a house on the earth without a foundation, against which the stream beat vehemently; and immediately it fell. And the ruin of that house was great. (Luke 6:46–49)

Reclaiming the Great Commission requires you to dig deep in order to create a stable foundation on which to build your community. Developing a Parish Health Plan requires you to formulate a strategy that is robust and true. Only then can the parish life that you build withstand the storms you face today and the ones that will inevitably come in the future.

Conclusion

"FATHER EVAN," my mentor said, "no one sits down and eats a salami in one meal. Rather, it is digested one thin slice at a time." This insightful and funny statement put me at ease. Until then, I had become increasingly anxious about the large number of things my parish needed to do to reclaim the Great Commission. My friend Chris reminded me that I didn't need to worry or try to accomplish what I was learning in one month, or even in one year. Instead, what I had to do was commit to taking one small step forward, knowing that over time I would make progress. My parish and I were learning to walk this road. I had to commit to the journey and the adventure Christ commissioned.

I still believe Jesus' last words to His apostles are essential to my identity as a Christian. My continued enthusiasm is found in the love I have for Jesus and what He taught and did. I am inspired by the beautiful and eternal truths He left to all of us—truths that have been passed on to me through His Church. As a result, I am still excited to tell people about Jesus. I am still excited by the adventure and the joy of sharing the gospel with others and helping them to join His Bride, the Church. I still believe that the greatest miracle is seeing a life transformed by the Good News of Jesus Christ within a community committed to making this transformation a reality.

I also remember how scared, overwhelmed, and ill-prepared I have felt in my time as a parish priest. And honestly, at times I still feel unsure of myself. I am often uncertain of my abilities, and I can feel inadequate for the continuous journey of reclaiming the Great Commission. Yet I know I must continue to set out on the road each day if I am to bring about greater health in myself and in my community.

This persistence has paid dividends. By God's grace I have become better equipped to face the challenges that present themselves. I have learned how to apply the lessons of the past to the situations of the present. With the help of others and the guidance of the Holy Spirit, I am better able to navigate the opportunities and pitfalls I face, and you will be too.

Additionally, I've learned that no one can go on this trip alone. To make this journey a success, we need help. Seeking it has been a blessing. Over time, I have worked with and learned from so many talented people—people who not only joined the journey and made it possible but enriched it along the way. Together we have grown in knowledge, skill, and strength. And as a result, I have enjoyed the journey more and more.

On my way to reclaiming the Great Commission, I have come to understand better my own weaknesses and how to deploy other people's strengths. I am still learning how to think more strategically. I am also continually learning how to articulate a mission and a vision and share them with those around me. Together we are making our way forward while recognizing we still have a long way to go.

Hopefully, as this journey continues, I am also learning to think less highly of myself. Humility is becoming a larger part of my walk with Christ and as a leader. It has also become increasingly apparent that the main reason for our community's achievements has been the contributions of others, while the failures and the responsibility for our setbacks are often mine.

On this journey, I am still learning how my pride and sense of accomplishment can become deadly obstacles. Pride is the enemy of both personal and parish health. Whenever it rears its ugly head, I stop learning, asking questions, and seeking a better tomorrow for myself and the community I serve.

But for those who wish to continue this journey, we take with us a growing desire to regain our sight, remember our lifesaving mission, prune what is dead, build bridges and take down barriers, while developing a sense of urgency for the work we do. And as we move forward, we work toward a shared definition of what it means to be a healthy parish, by seeking to share with one another and implement the four components of parish health: a commitment to Christ and the gospel, a commitment to connecting Christ and the gospel to our daily lives, a commitment to relationship building and forming a spiritual family, and operational excellence.

In doing this work, we identify and recognize the barriers that impede us—such as undeveloped leadership, leaders without a plan, unbalanced identity, resistance and sabotage, and stagnation. Finally, to reclaim the Great Commission, we recognize the importance of developing leadership in our communities at all levels. We then ask these same leaders to implement Parish Health Plans and establish Parish Health Teams that will move us toward our goal of reclaiming the Great Commission.

Of course, the window for this work may be closing for many of our parishes. This means leaders and members, like you, can no longer be complacent about your community's health if you hope to reverse the direction you are headed. You must act!

While there is much to be done, I am still encouraged, and you should be as well. I am encouraged because people like you love our Lord and His Church. You too have noticed that something must change. You are willing, like Abraham, to go where the Lord is guiding you: "Now the Lord said to Abram, Get out of your country, from your family and from your father's house, to a land that I will show you" (Gen. 12:1). You are willing to go on the journey of reclaiming the Great Commission. I know you will move heaven and earth to ensure that your parish's best days are ahead.

I still believe there is more to learn. Fortunately, you will discover new ways and additional resources we all can learn from, and you will add these to what I have shared here. My hope is that I have given you a solid starting place and stimulated a lifelong interest in the journey toward greater parish health for every church. Don't forget that the change we hope to see in our communities begins with a change in ourselves.

As I close, allow me to share again the words of our Lord that have encouraged people just like you to claim the Great Commission for almost two thousand years:

> And Jesus came and spoke to them, saying, "All authority has been given to Me in heaven and on earth. Go therefore and make disciples of all the nations, baptizing them in the name of the Father and of the Son and of the Holy Spirit, teaching them to observe all things that I have commanded you; and lo, I am with you always, *even* to the end of the age." Amen. (Matt. 28:18–20)

List of Resources

General Note

If you are interested in learning more about the subjects presented in this book as well as others to assist you on the journey to parish health, a variety of resources is available. I would encourage you to operate like a bee who flies about and collects nectar from various flowers, returning to the hive to make honey.

Non-print Resources

Coaching and Classes

Coaches and professional mentors can greatly accelerate your learning and development. It is likely that someone in your community is a coach or mentor or can recommend one. Additionally, many local community colleges and universities offer classes, both in person and online, on subjects such as leadership, decision-making, strategic planning, and organizational development and behavior.

Organizations

Many professional and parachurch organizations can help you reclaim the Great Commission, including those listed below. I also recommend that you check with your local clergy association, bishop, diocese, and archdiocese for direction and recommendations.

Orthodox Christian Leadership Initiative, www.orthodoxservantleaders. com.

Orthodox Natural Church Development, www.oncd.us.

For up-to-date information about the state of Orthodoxy in America, see www.orthodoxreality.org.

Podcasts

Listening to podcasts is another easy and effective way to grow and learn. Why not turn your drive time into a classroom? Once again, like a bee you need to choose carefully among the innumerable available podcasts. Talk to other people in your circle to see if they have a recommendation and conduct a careful search, reading reviews and listening for a few hours.

I suggest Michael Hyatt's podcasts, including *Lead to Win* and *The Orthodox Leader* on Ancient Faith Radio; and Bill Marianes's *Stewardship Calling,* also on AFR. Also, check the websites of the various Orthodox Christian archdioceses.

Books

From the innumerable books that could help your parish to reclaim the Great Commission, I have selected a few beneficial titles as well as a number of books recommended by people I trust.

Block, Peter. *Community: The Structure of Belonging.* Oakland, CA: Berrett-Koehler Publishers, 2018.

Bolsinger, Tod. *Canoeing the Mountains: Christian Leadership in Uncharted Territory.* Westmont, IL: IVP Books, 2018.

Brown, Brené. *Dare to Lead: Brave Work. Tough Conversations. Whole Hearts.* New York: Random House, 2018.

Collins, Jim. *Good to Great and the Social Sectors: Why Business Thinking Is Not the Answer.* New York: Harper, 2005.

Connors, Christopher D. *Emotional Intelligence for the Modern Leader: A Guide to Cultivating Effective Leadership and Organizations.* Emeryville, CA: Rockridge Press, 2020.

Covey, Stephen R. *The Seven Habits of Highly Effective People.* New York: Simon & Schuster, Anniversary ed., 2020.

Eisenhower, Susan. *How Ike Led: The Principles behind Eisenhower's Biggest Decisions*. New York: Thomas Dunne Books, 2020.

Haidt, Jonathan. *The Righteous Mind: Why Good People Are Divided by Politics and Religion*. New York: Vintage Books, 2013.

Heclo, Hugh. *On Thinking Institutionally*. Oxford: Oxford University Press, 2011.

Heifetz, Ronald, Marty Linsky, et al. *The Practice of Adaptive Leadership: Tools and Tactics for Changing Your Organization and the World*. Cambridge, MA: Harvard Business Review Press, 2009.

Kotter, John P. and Stan S. Cohen. *The Heart of Change: Real-Life Stories of How People Change Their Organizations*. Cambridge, MA: Harvard Business Review Press, 2012.

Kouzes, James M. and Barry Z. Posner. *A Leader's Legacy*. San Francisco: Jossey-Bass, 2006.

———. *The Leadership Challenge: How to Make Extraordinary Things Happen in Organizations*. San Francisco: Jossey-Bass, 2017.

Lee, Gus and Diane Elliott-Lee. *Courage: The Backbone of Leadership*. San Francisco: Jossey-Bass, 2006.

Lowney, Chris. *Everyone Leads: How to Revitalize the Catholic Church*. Lanham, MD: Rowman & Littlefield Publishers, 2017.

McLaren, Brian. *The Great Spiritual Migration: How the World's Largest Religion Is Seeking a Better Way to Be Christian*. Colorado Springs, CO: Convergent Books, 2017.

Phillips, Donald T. *Lincoln on Leadership: Executive Strategies for Tough Times*. Brentwood, TN: Warner Books, reprint, 1993.

Rainer, Thom S. *Autopsy of a Deceased Church: 12 Ways to Keep Yours Alive*. Nashville, TN: B&H Publishing, 2014.

Shitama, Jack. *Anxious Church, Anxious People: How to Lead Change in an Age of Anxiety*. Earleville, MD: Charis Works Inc., 2018.

White, Michael, and Tom Corcoran. *Rebuilt: Awakening the Faithful, Reaching the Lost, and Making Church Matter*. Notre Dame, IN: Ave Maria Press, 2013.

Acknowledgments

IT IS IMPOSSIBLE to recognize everyone who has contributed to this book. It is the result of the work, insights, and experiences of so many. I am grateful for the contributions they have made to my growth and to the ideas found here. I have benefited from the innumerable interactions and prayerful thoughts of countless parishioners, council members, ministry leaders, clergy, friends, authors, and podcasters. The cumulative impact of their pursuit of the Great Commission has changed me forever.

Specifically, I'd like to thank my mentor and friend Chris Christopher. Your commitment to my development is unique in my life. You have spent years helping to shape and guide me. I am thankful for your many suggestions, insightful questions, and the testing of each aspect of my writing. This book is immeasurably better because of you. To Stephanie Lindholm: Your loving support, edits, and gentle comments have improved this project in every respect. I will always be thankful for your willingness to talk through aspects of the book and for your encouragement to finish it. To Alexis Pappas: You have always supported me, and your enthusiastic contributions especially with the sections at the end of each chapter have improved the material being offered to our parishes. A special thanks also to Fr. Tom Tsagalakis, Fr. Peter Harrison, Fr. Nicholas Triantifilou, Fr. Dean

Talagan, Fr. Theodore Dorrance, Fr. Lou Christopulos, Dn. Paul Zaharas, Fr. Jim Kordaris, Fr. Jonathan Ivanoff, Dn. John Kavas, and Fr. Michael Tervo. Each of you has shared ideas with me and provided a living example of Christ. I am a better priest because of you. Your presence in my life through the years has deeply affected my mind and my soul.

To Jon and Maria Tschetter: Your constant support and friendship have been unwavering. No one can make this journey without true friends. To the founders of Saint Spyridon, the Brockhagen, Chacho, Harrison, Palmer, Tschetter, and Voegeli-Morris families: Your initial commitment to form Saint Spyridon cannot be forgotten. To Thomaida Hudanish: Your invitation to work on a presentation we titled "Reclaiming the Great Commission" first inspired me to collect the thoughts presented in this book. To Greg Drobny: Thanks for putting in your two cents and for your encouragement to try my hand at another book. To those who attended presentations I have made through the years on this topic: Your feedback and questions have pushed me to clarify and improve my thoughts.

To my editor Lynnette Horner from Ancient Faith Publishing: Your suggestions and careful review of this book have improved it beyond measure. Thank you. To John Maddex and the staff at AFP: Your continued encouragement has made it possible for me to add my little bit to the vast ocean of Christ's teaching.

Finally, and most importantly, I thank my family, whose love is unconditional. You are the best gifts God has given me, and I have learned more from each of you than I can express. I am a better person, husband, father, and priest because of you. I want to especially thank my wife, Presbytera Stacy, who read and reread this book. Your insights made it better. I am eternally grateful that God gave me such an incredible partner. I love you more today than yesterday but not as much as I will tomorrow. To my daughters Alexia, Eleni, and Maria:

Your skill with writing surpasses my own, and your interest in what I wrote was touching and inspiring. I am glad someone in this family knows where to place a comma. To Spyridon: I know you don't want to be a "priest-man," but your love for me and for Jesus makes me smile.

To God be the glory!

Father Evan Armatas is a parish priest in Loveland, Colorado, and has served the Church for over twenty years. He is the author of *Toolkit for Spiritual Growth: A Practical Guide to Prayer, Fasting, and Almsgiving* (Ancient Faith Publishing, 2020) and hosts a live call-in radio show on Ancient Faith Radio, *Orthodoxy Live*. Father Evan speaks across the US, and the ongoing questions and comments about his presentations on parish health inspired him to write this book. He and his wife, Presbytera Anastasia, are the happy parents of four.

We hope you have enjoyed and benefited from this book. Your financial support makes it possible to continue our non-profit ministry both in print and online. Because the proceeds from our book sales only partially cover the costs of operating **Ancient Faith Publishing** and **Ancient Faith Radio**, we greatly appreciate the generosity of our readers and listeners. Donations are tax deductible and can be made at **www.ancientfaith.com**.

To view our other publications,
please visit our website: **store.ancientfaith.com**

 ANCIENT FAITH RADIO

Bringing you Orthodox Christian music, readings, prayers, teaching, and podcasts 24 hours a day since 2004 at **www.ancientfaith.com**